Cameo Choices

Old Testament Teen Girls Speak to Teen Girls of Today

Tamara L. Knowles

TATE PUBLISHING & *Enterprises*

Cameo Choices
Copyright © 2008 by Tamara L. Knowles. All rights reserved.

No part of this publication may be reproduced, stored in a retrieval system or transmitted in any way by any means, electronic, mechanical, photocopy, recording or otherwise without the prior permission of the author except as provided by USA copyright law.

Scripture quotations marked "NKJV" are taken from *The New King James Version* / Thomas Nelson Publishers, Nashville: Thomas Nelson Publishers. Copyright © 1982. Used by permission. All rights reserved.

The opinions expressed by the author are not necessarily those of Tate Publishing, LLC.

Published by Tate Publishing & Enterprises, LLC
127 E. Trade Center Terrace | Mustang, Oklahoma 73064 USA
1.888.361.9473 | www.tatepublishing.com

Tate Publishing is committed to excellence in the publishing industry. The company reflects the philosophy established by the founders, based on Psalm 68:11,
"*The Lord gave the word and great was the company of those who published it.*"

Book design copyright © 2008 by Tate Publishing, LLC. All rights reserved.
Cover design by Jonathan Lindsey
Interior design by Lance Waldrop

Published in the United States of America
ISBN: 978-1-60799-005-5
1. Religion / Biblical Biography / Old Testament
2. Family & Relationships / Life Stages / Teenagers
08.12.08

This book is dedicated and committed to El Roi, my God and my Redeemer, for as you worked in my heart and mind, this book came into being. You have given so much to me; the desire of my heart is that this book will be solely to your honor and glory.

Table of Contents

9	Foreword
11	Introduction
13	Hagar
23	Lot's Daughters
33	Rebekah
47	Rachel and Leah
57	Dinah
67	Jephthah's Daughter
79	Tamar
87	Abishag
95	Naaman's Captive Girl
101	Esther
115	Chat Room

Foreword

Teenage girls today are faced with a multitude of difficult issues. They need love, support, and, most of all, spiritual help and direction from God's Word. Tamara and her husband, Cleve, have consistently been an encouragement to teenagers over the last twelve years as they have ministered in a Word of Life Teen Club in their local church and have applied biblical principles to these difficult problems.

In her book, Tamara has skillfully taken twelve girls from the Old Testament and looked at a portion of their lives. The "cameo portraits" reveal their difficulties, failures, and victories for the purpose of helping girls today deal with the challenges they face.

As we read through this book, we became more and more excited at the impact this will have on young ladies. This book can be an invaluable resource, not only for struggling teen girls, but also for those who are reaching out and ministering to them.

As Word of Life Missionary for Northern New England, it has been a privilege to witness Tamara's passion and compassion for impacting teens' lives, and her book reflects her heart.

Duane and Trish Gregory
Word of Life Local Church Ministries

Introduction

I have been given the privilege of working with teens for a number of years, and I have learned—if I didn't know already—that it is not easy being a teen. Not only are there physical transitions, but the accompanying dramatic swings of emotion that attend this physical transformation make even the smallest of incidents fraught with drama and tears, which wreak havoc in one's life. On top of that, it seems that many teens in this era are confronted with horrific choices—choices I, as a teen, never even thought of. Swamped by ungodly media and popular fashions, many teens are apparently influenced to mutilate their bodies and then hang themselves out for display. With drugs, smoking, and unstable homes, it's no wonder life seems more like a minefield or a bad dream instead of the stable, fulfilled, happy lives we all dream of. Confronted with constant decisions, do you ever wonder what God has to do with real life and if he really understands and cares?

Believe it or not, God does know what you're going through. Nothing has taken him by surprise! In fact, you will see in this book that he chose to insert the stories of other teen girls into the Old Testament of the Bible, cameo portraits of those who endured similar crisis situations: captivity, rape, teen pregnancy, betrayal. It's all there. Some girls handled the situations extraordinarily well, and we shall study how they survived, even thrived, in difficult circumstances. Other girls were sucked into situations where they laid themselves open to further sin, hurt, and consequences that have ricocheted down through the ages, even to today. We can learn from them what *not* to do and use their experiences as warning and guidance for our own choices.

The glimpses we see of these girls are as if God carved their silhouettes in the jewel of his Word: Simple, not too glaringly portrayed, but with sparse details that grant us a tantalizing view of teen girls caught in the tumult of their generation and culture, forced into gut choices that often were responses to situations not of their own making.

As you read of their lives from the perspective of their teen years and analyze their actions and situations, perhaps you will gain insights on how to survive—and thrive—in your own fraught choices. Perhaps someday, too, your own life will be shown as a select cameo portrait to other teens, displaying how you chose to live a life that glorified God so much that his glory catches your life in relief against the mundane plane of this life.

Most of all, I hope you'll come away seeing how relevant the Bible is to your own life. May you come to will know without a doubt the hope and trust in the God most of these girls served, who loves you above all things, and who is always in the know and in control.

Choosing His Glory,
Tamara Knowles

Hagar

Genesis 16

"Have I also here seen Him who sees me?"

Genesis 16:13b

There she sat, by a spring of water in the wilderness, a pregnant runaway with nothing but the clothes on her back. Alone, unloved, her absence hardly noticed—except that she wasn't back at the camp being tormented. Her initial anger and frustration had by this time spent itself, leaving Hagar empty and spent, prey to a multitude of questions. How had she gotten into this situation? It wasn't *her* fault that things had gotten so bad that she couldn't live there any longer—or was it? And as she sat there, taking a breather and wondering where to head to next, Hagar wondered how it was that she had landed into such a situation and where exactly things had gone wrong. Where had all this trouble begun, anyway?

Obviously, Hagar had given no thought to any possible negative future consequences when she'd been approached by her kind mistress earlier. In fact, Sarai and her husband had been good to her from the time she'd been acquired as a slave while Sarai and Abram were in Egypt, so why would she suspect that she was about to land herself in a whole lot of trouble? Perhaps it was because she'd been promoted to the position of being Sarai's personal servant that she knew all about the personal sorrow that Abram and Sarai shared. Here they had everything—so much wealth, in fact, that Abram's nephew, Lot, had to split away from them and find his own land, because the place where they camped was unable to provide for the abundance of flocks and herds. Here they were masters of their own lives, able to go where they wanted, guided by their personal God (or so her master believed), and yet they had a sorrow that had never been eased: they were childless.

It was even whispered around the compound that their master, Abram, had been promised by his God that he'd make a great nation out of his descendants. *Some god,* Hagar must've chortled quietly to herself, for here was Sarai, seventy-five years old, and still childless. *A bit ridiculous, really. What did that god expect Abram to do? Get another wife?* These thoughts might have been circling in Hagar's head as she viewed the situation from the perspective of an Egyptian, with her background of the Egyptian surplus of gods and the necessity of having to do everything for their deities. So when Sarai proposed that Abram get his heir through Hagar, well, it wasn't such a far-fetched idea to her; after all, it was pretty customary in the culture of their time. Besides, the fact that they also proposed that she'd be his wife too—imagine that! From slave to wife—such a tantalizing reward for a girl who'd only known a life of slavery thus far! So Hagar went along with this, a triangle suggested by Sarai herself, and agreed to by Abram. What harm could it do?

Hagar got pregnant quickly, and just as quickly the wrongness of the situation began to make itself known. She was like a body piercing gone wrong. Exotic. Desirable. Perfect until, all too soon, the rubbing and friction produced the angry redness of infection. Silly girl, she let her perceived status as young, pregnant, supposed wife number two (in contrast to old, barren wife number one, Sarai) go to her head. She grew prideful and spiteful, indicating to her erstwhile mistress every time she smoothed the gown over her growing belly that it was *she* who was fruitful, that it was *she* who was bearing the heir, not has-been, barren Sarai.

Hagar became a constant irritant until finally Sarai screamed at her husband, "My wrong be upon you" (Genesis 16:5a). Discord had grown between the couple, who'd been together through thick and thin, pulling up roots and heading for an unknown destination, going through a harrowing escape in Egypt, living the restless life of nomads. Life had not been perfect, but they'd gone through it together, just the two, husband and wife; and now, no longer two, but three, their previous harmony ruled no longer. Anger, insults, and blame echoed in their household, sending discord resonating through the camp.

Anger stripped away any pretence of fairness and equality, and the truth was out: they might have *said* she'd be his wife, but in reality Hagar was no more Abram's wife than any other concubine. In actuality, in the eyes of both Abram and Sarai, she was still Sarai's handmaid: "So

Abram said to Sarai, 'Indeed your maid is in your hand; do to her as you please'" (Genesis 16:6a). Poor Hagar. She had been a means to an end. Sarai found that their solution had been too painful after all and reality revealed that the means wasn't as important a person as Hagar had thought herself to be. All too soon she was made to regret her pride and haughtiness. With Abram's tacit permission, Sarai harshly responded to Hagar's proud behavior. Brought up short, young Hagar decided she couldn't take it one minute longer and ran way.

That's not so surprising. Things must've been pretty miserable, what with no one caring for her (remember, she was a foreigner, one of those Egyptians) and being reminded at every turn that she was nothing more than a pregnant servant. On top of that, the baby's father wasn't even standing up for her! Things must have seemed pretty grim to that young slave. Combine pregnancy hormones with teen hormones, and she probably wasn't thinking too clearly, deeming the awfulness of what she had been undergoing in camp to outweigh any danger that might lurk in the wilderness. Maybe she even thought it would serve her master right if his only child died because some wild animal got to her first. Maybe she subconsciously hoped that she would be missed and he'd come looking for her, reinstating her as an person in his eyes. Whatever she was thinking, it wasn't surprising that she ran. Indeed, the amazing thing was *not* that Hagar ran away, but that she came back—on her own.

She came back, yet the Hagar who returned was not the same Hagar who had fled in anger and bitterness.

She came back quieter, humbler, submissive—a changed creature. She was still pregnant and still party to an awkward situation, but soon it became apparent to all who lived in that small community that the prideful and abrasive slave who had fled returned as a servant who was willing to submit to the hand of her mistress. The horrible mess was still there, but somehow Hagar had learned to live *in* the situation.

How did this change happen? What gave her the courage to come back and submit to whatever was handed to her? Simply put, when she sat down to rest by that well in the wilderness, she met one whom she called "El Roi," which, when literally translated, means "You-Are-the-God-Who-Sees" (Genesis 16:13). There she learned that the God whom her master worshipped and served was a personal God, one who knew her and saw her plight. She learned not only that he was so much more than any god she had known in her homeland, but also that her master's God had plans for even her. And the one who ran away aimlessly in despair was given a hope, direction, and a purpose—something to work and live for.

The hope God gave her was that she was indeed pregnant with a *son,* and that son would have a great future. Joined with that hope was the purpose of not only surviving, but of doing what was best for her son, which was to return to her master and mistress. To return to them would thus give him a better chance of survival than wandering around in the wilderness, prey to any predator, man, or beast.

Additionally, the direction given her by "You-Are-the-God-Who-Sees" was that she was to return to her mistress and she was to *submit* to her mistress. Dump the attitude. Accept the situation. In other words, she was to obey and do whatever her mistress, Sarai, wanted. It was a tall order involving a huge attitude adjustment. Somehow, knowing that she had met the God Who Sees made such an impact on her that she did just that: she returned, she submitted, and, in time, her son, Ishmael, was born.

That is not to say that the situation became any easier for her. That triangle should never have been formed, but because it was, each individual had to live with the consequences of that foolish decision. Sarai had a daily reminder that her husband had slept with another woman, and to swallow the fact that their lack of children was indeed because she was the problem. Abram was to live in the discomfort of knowing he'd done something that was displeasing to God and hurt his wife. Additionally, he couldn't take full pleasure in the only child he had, because to do so would hurt Sarai more. Hagar had to live in a no-man's land of being not exactly a servant but not fully a wife either. She was the foreigner in the midst of a close-knit community, tolerated only because she was the mother of Abram's only child. Life was not easy; she lived for the love of her son and submitted. Thus, a decision formulated to fix a problem their own way caused great pain and discomfort, yet all three learned to live with the situation until God took care of the problem in his own way—but that's another story.

Is there anything that can be learned from Hagar's

mistakes? Was there a point in the situation when Hagar could have said, "Whoa, this doesn't look right—better not go there"? Probably not, simply because she was Sarai's slave and thus obligated to fall in with her wishes. The burden of guilt in that triangle was on her master and mistress, not her. Still, note that it doesn't matter if everyone supposedly says getting involved in an affair is okay and to go along with what "everyone else" is doing. It is never right to get involved with a married man. Never. Period. To get involved in an extramarital affair will only cast unnecessary baggage and pain on all involved, whether a child results or not. Don't do it.

Okay, so Hagar was involved, and the deed was done. What went wrong next? Hagar was young, and she wasn't very wise. Not only did she let her new status go to her head, but also she had the temerity to tease and taunt and torment the one who had provided her with this new opportunity. Rather than being grateful for the elevation of status and the means by which her future was to be cared for, because she was the mother of her master's future heir, Hagar thoughtlessly ground at the wound of barrenness that Sarai had carried for countless years, mercilessly underscoring any thoughts of uselessness and poor self-image Sarai might have harbored as year by year she remained barren. Her nasty attitude so aggravated the situation that at last Sarai reached the point where she had to get rid of that exotic, ungrateful, conceited upstart at any cost. The beautiful solution had become an inflamed wound of putrid illness in their household.

Hagar didn't have to be that nasty irritant. She *chose* to

behave the way she did. If she had chosen to humble herself in the first place and kept her mouth shut, she would have spared herself, Sarai, and Abram a whole lot of heartbreak. As she found, to her regret, however, it is all too easy to get wrapped in the situation and lose a proper perspective of how things really are. It would have been far better if she had sat back, watched, and listened, and then sought for a place in that household where she could've been a help, not a problem. In any situation you, as a teen, are plunged into, whether it is a problem of your own making or someone else's bad situation, it doesn't help to add to that problem by allowing your perspective to be skewed by emotion. Choose to sit back, think the problem through, keep your mouth shut, and work at being a help instead of a problem. Additionally, don't, like Hagar, demean someone and cut another down just to make yourself feel good. Rather, look for ways to encourage others, thus making any bad situation a shade easier.

Above all, Hagar didn't know how to deal with the situation because she just didn't know the one who was to later change her life. When Hagar met the one true God, whom she had called "You-Are-the-God-Who-Sees," not only was her attitude and behavior changed, but she was able to live within the situation (something she had earlier thought to be impossible to do). Do you know the God-Who-Sees? David, the writer of many of the Psalms in the Bible, said of him, "The Lord is near to those who have a broken heart, and saves such as have a contrite spirit" (Psalm 34:18). In whatever situation you are in or thinking to be involved in, wouldn't you like to know the God who not only knows you—"O Lord, You have searched me and known me" (Psalm 139:1)—but who is willing to be with you and to direct and guide you in every way? To those who follow him, he says, "I will instruct you and teach you in the way you should go; I will guide you with My eye" (Psalm 32:8). This same God has also said of himself, "Fear not, for I am with you; Be not dismayed, for I am your God. I will strengthen you, Yes, I will help you, I will uphold you with My righteous right hand" (Isaiah 41:10). Wouldn't you like to know the God who changed Hagar's life, too?

If you already know him, when was the last time you asked him for help? When did you last bother to open the Bible to find out what he's trying to tell you? Come to him, and in him you will find forgiveness for what you've done (if you're really, really sorry you did it), and through him you'll find a way to live through the situation. God came to Hagar, and her life was totally changed. Are you ready to have him change yours too?

Hagar was a minor character in a major situation, yet what she got involved in had huge consequences. Her participation spiraled into a situation beyond her control, causing great misery to herself and Abram and Sarai, and the situation that developed between her son and the promised son Sarai finally bore has an impact that still resonates today in our current events. She could not have known where her decisions were leading her, but in the midst of that turmoil and pain, she could have chosen to live in such a way that the immediate repercussions could have been a whole lot easier to live with. She didn't, but later on, through her, we are shown that there is an all-seeing God who can transform lives. That same God knows you too. Do you know him?

Lot's Daughters

Genesis 19:30–38

"I have two daughters who have
not known a man …"

Genesis 19:8a

They lost everything—their home, family, lifestyle, status—everything except their father, a small consolation for their loss in their eyes. Life was reduced to primitive survival, their luxurious home replaced by a dank, dark cave where their cowardly father had exiled them. It had happened so fast. One day they'd been living luxuriously, doing whatever they wanted, and then these two mysterious "guys" had come and literally dragged them out of town—their mom, dad, and them, the only two unmarried girls still under their father's authority. Then it was a mad dash of inarticulate, throat-searing terror as they staggered on, fearing for their very lives. It was only after entering Zoar with the hairs on the backs of their necks seared by the scorching rain of fire and brimstone, which was melting out of existence their town and home, that the realization hit them that their mom was no longer with them, another casualty of God's judgment.

Their father, well, he'd lost everything too, including the rank and status that had come with the wealth he'd so enjoyed. The girls had seen him sitting in the town gates, moralizing against the depravity that surrounded him. They'd watched him attempt to get his sons-in-law to take him seriously when danger loomed, failing thoroughly, yet wavering in dismay so long that those mysterious strangers had literally grabbed their arms and hustled them out of town. Surviving the holocaust, Lot's daughters then watched their father become a nervous wreck. Stripped of status and the authority of wealth, sole survivors of the catastrophe that had wiped out two significant cities, Lot saw danger in every corner, a threat on the face of anyone who approached. So he ran again, this time to the caves in the mountains, where the angels had originally suggested they go.

Bereft, bitter, and lonely, these two girls latched on to the one thing they wanted and single-mindedly went for it. Never mind that they used and abused their father, took advantage of his weaknesses, and stripped the honor from a man who had lost everything except his tattered integrity.

The problem, as seen from their point of view, was that in their isolation there was no hope of marriage, children, or a home. Stated with mock concern, "Our father is old, and there is no man on the earth to come in to us as is the custom of all the earth" (Genesis 19:31b). Note the hysterical exaggeration: no man on the earth at *all?*

Their solution? "It's easy," said sister one to sister two. "Let's get Dad so drunk that he loses all his inhibitions …" and with a narcissist's single-minded purpose, the two girls proceeded to trample all taboos against incest and demolished any pretext of filial honor and duty. In the process of time, both daughters became mothers, each delivering a son. These two boys eventually became the "fathers" of the Moabites and the Ammonites, two tribes that, generations later, became a constant harassment and threat to the fledgling country of Israel.

Frankly, the tale of the treachery of these two girls is not generally dwelt on. Sermons on the wickedness of Sodom and Gomorrah, about Lot's wife looking back and becoming a pillar of salt, even about Lot's love of wealth and status and ultimate rescue abound. His daughters … well, they're mentioned as a small sideline, if anything. The story about these incestuous girls is not pretty and not something for "tender" ears, yet there is something more that can be learned from them beyond the facts of how the nations of Ammon and Moab came into existence. In fact, the story of these two teenagers is very appropriate for teens and parents today, seen in the situation they endured, how they handled it, and why they were willing to go to the extreme they did.

First, they were victims and survivors of a devastating act of God. Now consider the hurricanes, floods, earthquakes, ice storms, and other natural disasters prevalent today that could be looked upon as literal acts of God. Second, having been flung into a situation alien to their upbringing and filled with grief, these teenagers comforted themselves using anything they could, a technique not unknown among teens today. Skewed morality, drugs, alcohol, smoking, cutting, and extreme body piercing are just some of the things teens sometimes do to help them forget the nightmare of what they're going through. A further similarity is that, disturbingly, today there is a rising issue of narcissism—extreme self-centeredness—which was also embodied in the behavior of these two girls. Yes, they'd been through great trauma and lost everything, but instead of nurturing and comforting each other and lifting up grateful hearts to God for their rescue, they only saw their "need" and ruthlessly used their dad to satisfy it. Broken down into these separate issues, is it not obvious that the story of Lot's daughters is loaded with valuable warnings for teens and their parents today?

The huge question that jumps out at any morally sane person is, how did these two girls get to the point where they were able to justify in their minds an act that violated a taboo that was observed by any decent human being? What contributed to their warped inner morality so that when faced with a problem, they came up with a skewed solution?

First and foremost, when stripped of all superficialities and thrust into unfamiliar territory, these two girls fell back on the lessons they had ingrained in them while growing up—not lessons told them by their parents, but what they had seen and heard and been shown repeatedly, day by day, by those around them. For years Lot's daughters had lived in and among the citizens of a city that was so morally rotten that God had to *burn* its existence off the face of the earth, as if to cauterize the diseased sore of vileness. Daily they had witnessed their father's ineffectual morality balanced against the colorful and amoral society of Sodom. Although unwed themselves and, it is assumed, virgins, they watched and listened and learned from what went on around them, witnessing the warped behaviors of neighbors, friends, and acquaintances (you name it, it probably was there) on a day-to-day basis. Is it any wonder, then, that a little incest might not have been such a big deal to them?

Another factor that contributed to the complete self-centeredness demonstrated by the girls when they single-mindedly pursued their goal can be traced back to their previous lifestyle and status. Not that every individual brought up in wealth is selfish, but, by and large, it is a problem. Lot had been forced to be separated from his uncle, Abraham, because, between the two of them, the land could not support the wealth of livestock they owned. So Lot had settled in the lush and fruitful valley, where his wealth bought him prestige and comfort, this being evidenced by the fact that he was sitting in the gate of the city (a sign of status) when the two angels approached the entranceway. Consider, too, that these two girls were Lot's youngest daughters, the last two unmarried girls in his family. Combine wealth with being the youngest of a large family and it doesn't take much to imagine that they were the loved, pampered darlings, given anything their hearts desired, able to wrap their father around their little fingers. Scripture doesn't state that they were spoiled, but given the ease with which they simply took what they wanted as older girls, it's plausible.

Finally, the two girls were willing to use their father, ruthlessly manipulating and utilizing his weaknesses because, when it came right down to it, they had no respect for authority, especially that of their father. Things about their father didn't match up in their eyes. He was supposedly a moral man, yet he had chosen to live in a cesspool of sin. He was a man of status, yet no one took him seriously. Note how none of their siblings and their siblings' spouses had heeded his warning to flee. Although protected by God and divinely rescued, he cravenly fled from the town of Zoar and hid in the mountains because he was afraid of men. Although he was a big man when he was surrounded by his wealth, when that was all stripped away, what was left was a shell of the man they had known growing up. And, as teens so often do, his daughters considered him to be weak and hypocritical, so they discounted his feelings and what he believed in and orchestrated the events that must have torn him apart when he came out of the drunken stupors and found out that his daughters had been impregnated by him.

Scriptures tell us about real people, people we can learn from, either from what they did right or what they did wrong. The story of Lot's daughters is not simply to relate how the nations of Ammon and Moab were founded, but their conduct can caution and teach teens and parents today.

Test yourself. Do you have a problem with any of the issues these two girls struggled with? Selfishness, lack of filial respect, or finding that you're involved in messed-up ways of handling the "stuff" you're going through, like cutting, anorexia, or loose morality? Be honest with yourself. No one is accusing you of being totally messed up, but maybe, just maybe, this could help you see the problem and start working on the cure.

Step one in stopping the bleeding is that you need a moral starting point. By moral, I am pointing you to the only way you can completely be freed from the bondage of the habits you're involved in or are starting to be involved in. You need to have a relationship with Jesus Christ. He said, "Most assuredly, I say to you, whoever commits sin is a slave of sin. And a slave does not abide in the house forever, but a son abides forever. Therefore if the Son makes you free, you shall be free indeed" (John 8:34b-36). He also said, "I have come that they might have life and they may have it more abundantly" (John 10:10b), and, "I am the way, the truth, and the life. No one comes to the Father except through Me" (John 14:6b).

==Only through Jesus Christ will you be able to acknowledge, confront, and be released from any cycle of self-destruction.== Think of what he did for us to give us that freedom. To free all of us from the bondage of sin, Jesus Christ, the only begotten Son of God, came to this earth wrapped in the frail human frame, lived a sinless life, yet died a horrible death, condemned by false accusations. He, dying sinless, took our sins upon him so that, losing his earthly life, we might have eternal life.

His shed blood guarantees our forgiveness from sin and release from the bondage of sin, but his resurrection from the dead guarantees our eternal life with him: "I have been crucified with Christ; it is no longer I who live, but Christ lives in me; and the life which I now live in the flesh I live by faith in the Son of God, who loved me and gave himself for me" (Galatians 2:20). Tell him that you believe that he died for you, ask him to forgive you your sins, and accept his gift of eternal life and freedom from being bound by the "have-to" of sin. Forevermore, as you grow in your walk with him by reading the Bible, his Word, you will discover that you not only know what not to do, but you will also have help doing what should be done because he will always be there for you. Now that's a good foundation for getting out of the relentless hurricane of sin that has sucked you in, isn't it?

If you already are a child of God (or have just made that decision) and you have God's moral standards to live by, the next thing that needs to be controlled is what and with whom you surround yourself. Lot's daughters lived in an environment steeped in wrongness. They watched and heard about the goings-on around them, and eventually the morals (or lack thereof) was reflected in what they did to their dad. The same goes for every one of us. We need to be very careful about what we fill our minds with, for Scripture says,

> Finally, brethren, whatever things are true, whatever things are noble, whatever things are just, whatever things are pure, whatever things

> are lovely, whatever things are of good report,
> if there is any virtue and if there is anything
> praiseworthy—meditate on these things.
>
> Philippians 4:8

What we fill our minds with will eventually become ingrained into every fiber of our being, so be very careful what you read, watch, do, or who you hang around with. ==The brain is an awesome organ, soaking up a whole lot more than you think.==

As has been mentioned, Lot's daughters also had a problem with selfishness. Most of us have a problem with selfishness. That's why in Zechariah 7:6, the Israelites were condemned because, among other things, they were selfish: "When you eat and when you drink, do you not eat and drink for yourselves?" What should we do instead? First Corinthians 10:23 says, "Let no one seek his own, but each one the other's well-being." More specifically, according to Philippians 2:4, we are to "let each of you look out not only for his own interests, but also for the interests of others." Pretty straight talk, isn't it? How do we not let selfishness become a disease? First, ask God to help you follow him first and consider others next. Then, you practice, practice, and practice some more, putting the needs of others before your own. Learning to do so will pay you back with more dividends than you will ever imagine, both in your relationships with others and for your future in heaven.

The last lesson that the girls inadvertently teach us

is that even if you don't think your father deserves your respect (dads are people too, and they do make mistakes), you still *must*. Ephesians 6:2 very clearly tells us that children are to "honor your father and mother, which is the first commandment with promise." Honor your parents because you are supposed to, not because you want to. It is a choice to make and act on, especially now, as you may be changing and developing ideas that don't always agree with what your parents think. If Lot's daughters had chosen to honor their dad in their thoughts and actions, those acts of incest would never have happened, and they would not have been added to the hall of infamy in Scripture. Best of all, there would never have been the nations of Ammon and Moab to be a pain to Israel in years to come.

Known by nothing more than "Lot's daughters," these two girls went through a horrible upheaval and lost just about everything they knew and cared for. There's no question that the tragedy they underwent may have caused them to become unhinged, yet beyond a doubt, when everything is ripped away, what's left is what has been ingrained in a person. They chose to act out of their selfishness and in the process treated their father as if he were a mere possession, to be used and abused and thrown away. Theirs was a choice. What you choose to do with your life, well, you're living it right now; it's up to you what you decide to do with it.

Rebekah

Genesis 24

"I will go." Genesis 24:58c

As her hometown wavered out of her view due to the heat waves that shimmered across the semi-arid land, Rebekah had plenty of time to review in her heart and mind the incredible events of the past twenty-four hours. Homesickness vied with anticipation; being alternately replaced by a sudden desire to kick herself for so recklessly throwing away a safe and predictable life in favor of an unknown, rich, and distant husband. Was she crazy, or was she truly following the path a powerful God had ordained for her? How awesome was it that she, of all people, was the one and only perfect choice for this unknown heir of her wealthy uncle? Yet what on earth had possessed her to offer to quench the thirst of the camels that accompanied the mysterious stranger? Hour after hour, as her camel plodded on endlessly, gently swayed and jerked by its off-rhythmic stride, Rebekah shook her head at herself time and again as she sorted through all the impressions, discussions, and actions that had set her on this irreversible path to an unfamiliar future.

Young, beautiful, single, and part of a financially secure family, her friends had often enviously voiced their opinions that Rebekah was lucky, that she had everything going for her. She hadn't argued, for in her culture, her life *was* all sewn up and set to follow the predictable lines of any young, wealthy, beautiful girl: marriage then a family of her own. Most likely, she probably wouldn't even have to move too far away from her comfortable home in Nahor, Mesopotamia. Hard to believe, Rebekah mused, that as she had plodded day by day in the safe routine of the known (much like her camel was now endlessly plodding), she hadn't had even an inkling that her safe and predictable future was destined to be challenged dramatically by a dusty, tired servant who blew in from nowhere.

Her day had started just like any other day, with the same old routine and the same old chores she had done since she had been strong enough to shoulder the water amphora for the daily excursions to the town well. As the dusk softened the walls of her home, Rebekah had hitched up the vessel for yet another trip to the water supply, soon to be joined by her chattering girlfriends as they trekked down to the well together. The daily routine gave no warning of the upset coming her way. She simply was doing what she always did and was her usual self: generous, impulsive, compassionate, considerate of others, helpful ... (Note that all these characteristics were already part of her prior to the fateful meeting with the soon-to-be herald of an exotic dilemma.) Could it be that God had already been working in her life years before this fateful moment, raising her up and grooming her for the role she was about to play?

Little did she know how perfectly she fit the bill of her uncle Abraham's requirements for a wife for his son. After revealing himself to Rebekah and her family, Abraham's servant had shared extensively with them what had transpired between him and his master at his journey's start—how her uncle, the patriarch Abraham, was nearing the end of his life, so since his son was unwed, he wanted to make sure his son and heir, Isaac, would marry the right kind of girl. Of paramount importance, Abraham had thought, was that his son's wife would be one who was of his own kin from his old homeland. He wanted his son to have nothing to do with the heathen women of the land he lived in with their foreign gods and traditions, so his most trusted servant was granted the task of seeking this wife from Abraham's homeland, over six hundred miles away, a clearly daunting task, shown by the servant's protest: "Perhaps the woman will not be willing to follow me to this land" (Genesis 24:5b).

Abraham's reply had been twofold: One, the Lord God would send before him an angel (in other words, this was all under God's control); and two, there was the possibility that the woman *would* refuse to come. If such was the case, Abraham had assured his servant that he, the servant, would then be released from his obligation of finding this mysterious woman for his master's son.

Rebekah, as she reviewed in her mind Abraham's answer, was floored yet again by the knowledge that Uncle Abraham possessed such a confidence in his God that he was certain that God would definitively reveal to the servant who that special person was! As she looked ahead to her unknown future, day running into endless day as they traversed the changing geography of the land, Rebekah often found it to be a comfort, knowing that even if she was the "perfect one," she hadn't been forced to come, that she had indeed been faced with choice and that her uncle had known that.

Rebekah then rewound her thoughts back to that quiet, warm evening at the well. As she and her friends neared the well, she really hadn't been expecting anything spectacular to happen while doing her chores. Once at the well, however, while waiting her turn to draw up the water, Rebekah's eyes were drawn to a stranger sitting quietly by the well. He looked dusty, tired, yet expectant, somehow removed from the chaos of chattering girls and bellowing camels (it was obvious that the camels belonged to his entourage, for they were just as dusty as he was). Little did she know that this man, Abraham's servant, having arrived at his destination but being unsure what his next move was to be and how he was to find the right bride, was at that moment asking for a sign from God. Specifically, he prayed that if he asked a young woman for a drink, the right woman would not only willingly succor his need but would also volunteer to slake the thirst of his camels. (This was an extraordinary request, for a thirsty camel can drink up to thirty gallons of water in just a few minutes! Multiply that by ten ... A girl who volunteered to take up such a task would have to be out of the ordinary—or crazy!)

While the prayer was still in his heart (he later told Rebekah and her family) God answered it, for as he prayed, he noticed the concerned and curious look on Rebekah's face as she attended to her chore. When she straightened from drawing up the water and turned to make her way back home with her filled pitcher, the servant then made an instant decision and, going over to her, asked her for a drink ... To this day, she couldn't explain what prompted her to offer to water the camels too. Sure, she was tenderhearted and hated to see animals suffer, but it was an enormous task. It was an impulsive decision, but one that unleashed the runaway events that were soon to flip her world upside down.

Immediately after she completed her Herculean task of watering the camels, the formerly dumfounded and silent servant whipped into action. First he bestowed upon the perspiring and bewildered Rebekah golden jewelry, all the while plying her with questions about herself, about her family, and whether her home would be able to provide food and lodging for him and his escort. Innocently she revealed her family line, generously she offered her family's hospitality, and unwarily she thus smoothed the path of Abraham's servant's quest.

The servant could not contain himself, for she was a distant niece of his master, exactly the person he'd been sent to look for! Before the bemused girl, he immediately stopped to worship and glorify the God of his master, Abraham, who had so gloriously and specifically answered his prayer. Perhaps the mention of her kinsman Abraham's name spurred her into action, making her realize that somehow this man was on a mission that was related to her family (though she still hadn't hit upon the idea that this whole mission revolved around her), but somehow this resilient young lady then managed to find the strength to run home and pour out the story of the unusual encounter to her family and to warn them of the unexpected guests.

Events rapidly unfolded. After Rebekah had told her family what had happened, showed them her jewelry, and warned them that the man and his retinue were on their way over, her brother, Laban, immediately took off and ran back to the servant (still standing by the well as his servants prodded the reluctant camels back into order) and formally backed up Rebekah's invitation, leading them to their home.

The events that followed were hard for Rebekah to order in her mind; everything had gained such a sense of urgency, with one thing following on the heels of another. She soon realized that although the servant and his escort were quickly housed, made comfortable, and offered food, it was obvious that the man himself had something on his mind. Radiating excitement and a sense of urgency, he had even refused the food for himself but instead begged to reveal his errand immediately to these kinfolk of his master, Abraham.

Rebekah wasn't actually in the room at the time, but later she was told how the servant rapidly, and in sequence, shared the details of Abraham's wealth, need, and his own errand: to bring back for Abraham's heir a wife from his own people. Then he told of how Rebekah had been a direct fulfillment of his prayer to God—down to the last exact detail. (The first time Rebekah heard this story, she couldn't believe that her brother wasn't making up the story, but then again, the old man *had* acted as if she'd offered him the whole world, the way he had accepted her offer to water the camels.) What, Laban asked her, as he told her the story, could they possibly have said? They could see God's handiwork; how dare they go against the hand of God? Could they—would they—deny their kinsman's request? Of course not. Since it was customary to arrange marriages anyhow, it seemed like this would be a good idea, landing Rebekah a good husband with the right family without even trying. A further consideration in favor of the plan was they'd be reeling in a good dowry. They granted the request, and Rebekah's future was assured.

Elated with his quick success, the servant again praised God and then made haste to shower Rebekah and her family with more rich gifts, gifts of gold and silver jewelry and rich clothing, gifts that tactfully underscored to the family the truth of his master's extreme wealth. Worn out from the trip, released from the anxiety of meeting his master's requirements, relieved that everything was going according to plan, all these elements soon sent the old man to bed after he'd finally eaten, to sleep the sleep of a man in peace.

That's not to say that Rebekah slept, however. How could she? Faced with such a momentous opportunity, she wondered that she even slept at all! Every action, every word, each detail of conversation, the richness of the gifts—all these had been whirling in her mind as she had sleeplessly reviewed the servant's story, looking for any note of falseness and wondering if what had just occurred was real or part of an incredible dream. A teensy bit of rebellion about having her life thus summarily taken care of without her say-so, jangled with a hint of uneasiness about the idea of leaving behind all that was familiar.

Then the element of romance, of meeting a rich, mysterious stranger was soon supplanted with qualms about the man himself. Was he kind? Was he handsome? Would he be patient with her, as she would have so much to learn, transitioning from an urban lifestyle to that of a nomad? Would she be able to handle the disparity between her current and future lifestyle? Would it be worth it, or would she spend a life of regrets and yearning for home and predictability? Was she about to make a big mistake? Filtering through and around the tumult in her mind was a little awe that she had been, and was, an important detail in the plans of an awesome and powerful God. Somewhere in the midst of that realization, Rebekah fell asleep—finally.

Next morning Rebekah had woken, bleary-eyed, into an uproar. Apparently, fully satisfied at having achieved his goal of finding the perfect bride, promptly upon getting up the next morning, Abraham's servant had shocked Rebekah's family by pressing them to allow him to depart immediately with Rebekah. Perhaps he was afraid that if he gave them too much time, they might think twice about allowing this daughter and sister to move so far away. *But maybe,* Rebekah later charitably wondered, *maybe the reality of Uncle Abraham's advanced age and impending death was pressing heavily on his conscience.* Not surprisingly, the idea didn't go over too well. Giving permission for her to get married was one thing, but to allow her to be whirled away before they even had a chance to get used to the idea of her leaving was preposterous! What about finishing her trousseau or her wedding clothes? She wouldn't even be able to take the time to say good-bye to all her friends and family members. It was too hasty, they had protested.

Even as Rebekah's family protested about the haste, their denials had battered uselessly at the old man's determination. Eventually his stubborn persistence wore down their arguments, as he emphasized again and again how blatantly this was a part of God's plans. Battered by his enthusiasm, they had finally relented, weakly saying, "We will call the young woman and ask her personally" (Genesis 24:57). Maybe they thought there was no way a young girl would consent to be swept away abruptly, almost secretly, with no fanfare or good-bye parties or wedding showers. Really, there she was, not only entering a new phase in her life, but preparing to say good-bye to everything that was familiar, being pretty much guaranteed that she'd never see any of her family and friends again—ever. *It was inevitable,* Rebekah's family had thought, even hoped, *that she would balk at this sudden departure.*

Would Rebekah indeed be willing? This was the time for her momentous choice on which everything hung: it was all up to her. Would she be willing to drop everything and leave immediately with no time to pack, say good-bye to friends, and have second thoughts? Would she indeed be willing to trade the known for the unknown; to leave her family, likely never to see them again; to exchange a comfortable urban lifestyle for the nomadic lifestyle of living in tents? Was she willing to trust this servant's word that this unknown, unseen man was indeed the perfect spouse for her, knowing nothing about him—not even his name—except that he was the son of Abraham, heir to great wealth? That could have been a time when she could have objected or chosen to nurse a grudge about being used and abused, but she hadn't.

Standing at this crossroad in her life, Rebekah had made her choice: "I will go" (Genesis 24:58c), three words that would transform her life completely. And off they went.

And here I am, Rebekah said to herself, drawing her thoughts back into the present as they neared their destination. Questions still plagued her, even as she plodded day by day on her camel toward her chosen future. *What will the future be like?* She asked herself. *Will I continue to have this deep peace that I've done the right thing? Will the deep certainty I carry within that the God my uncle Abraham worships is still in control and able to carry me through whatever is in store for me? Will I, even a young, insignificant girl, be able to fully know this awesome God whom my uncle apparently knows so well? There are so many questions awaiting answers!*

Suddenly, distracted from her inner turmoil, Rebekah noticed that they were approaching a sizeable cluster of tents, while beyond the encampment, she could see extensive flocks of goats and sheep milling with other livestock under the watchful gaze of the herdsmen in the distance. As the scene gradually came into greater focus when they drew nearer, Rebekah abruptly realized that outside the camp's parameters, an observer was standing in the fields, a man who stood immovable, staring at their approaching cavalcade, his eyes apparently riveted on her. Abruptly he then started to walk toward them, his path intersecting with their route. When they reached the compound, as Rebekah dismounted from her camel, she asked her escort, "Who is this man walking in the field to meet us" (Genesis 24:65b)? His answer took her breath away. "It is my master" (Genesis 24:65c).

His master! My future husband? Now is the time. Now I will discover for sure whether I've done the right thing in trusting God for my direction. Taking a deep breath, Rebekah took up her veil and covered herself modestly as she waited to meet the man who was to be her husband.

When one considers Rebekah and the incredible choice she made, many questions hauntingly tease one. Rebekah threw away a life of stability and security for one that was uncertain and unknown, making her hasty decision based on the say-so of an old servant, his testimony of his God's answered prayer.

==Why was she willing to go?== What made her so certain that this was the right thing for her? Was it the lure of greater wealth? Was she in love with the concept of marriage, swept away by the romance of it all? Was she bored with her same ole, same ole lifestyle and grasped this as an opportunity to escape? Or did she perceive that it was a done deal and that she might as well get it over with?

Any of those reasons would have left her floundering in regrets and indecision two hours down the road. No, she needed something more concrete on which to base her decision—something that would carry her through mile after mile of uncertainty as they plodded through the wilderness on that six hundred-plus-mile journey back to Abraham. She needed something that would carry her through the inevitable homesickness and the pains and sufferings that she would have to deal with so far from home, and Mom and Dad, and all that had been familiar as she adjusted to a new home, lifestyle, culture, and customs. Hebrews 11:1 says, "Now faith is the substance of things hoped for, the evidence of things unseen." Could it be that she had that faith? That she was willing to entrust her life and future into the hands of this living God of Abraham's? Indeed, it is only with faith in God Almighty that she could make such a momentous decision, forsaking all else but following the path of God's making.

Decision making is an integral part of life. Some people find it easy to make decisions, while others agonize as they stand at the perceived crossroads in their lives. As a teen today, you have many such decisions: to smoke or not to smoke, or do drugs, or "go all the way," or do what your friends are pressuring you to do. How do you make the right decisions that can help you choose a path pleasing to God in this crazy, mixed-up world? Such choices are not new. We've seen from the story in Genesis 24 how this teenage girl, Rebekah, was faced with an incredible crossroad that was destined to transform her life. She chose to follow what she knew to be the direction of God for her life and never, to our knowledge, looked back.

What about you? Is God calling you toward a certain direction, career, boyfriend, or spouse? How about the "little" decisions you have to make? What are you depending on to help you choose what is right, pure, and good for you? At what crossroads are you standing? Not everything is as drastic as what Rebekah faced, but indeed every decision needs to have good reasoning behind it. Rebekah's was her belief that she could trust God to carry her through. Are you willing to have faith in that same God, to trust that he knows what is best for you and that what he tells you to do in his Word, the Bible, would be for your own good? Can you trust him to lead you down the unknown path? Can you let him have control of your life? Are you able to follow the path that you know God is leading you to, even if it is uncertain and scary and unknown? Are you willing to say by faith, like Rebekah, "I will go," or, in your own life, "I will obey"? Can you choose to follow his direction as Rebekah did?

Rachel and Leah

Genesis 29

"Why then have you deceived me?"

Genesis 29:25d

Sibling rivalry can be devastating. Witness the relationship between Leah and Rachel. Theirs is a story of two sisters whose interactions were uneasy but stable, until their romantic cousin, Jacob, appeared on the scene—the catalyst that stirred the situation into a messy cauldron of deception and betrayal.

Leah had very little in common with her younger sister, Rachel. Not only did the years separate the two, but also their vocations. Even their looks seemed to emphasize their polarity. Genesis 29 includes a few descriptive details of the sisters, sparse in words but pregnant with implications. Rachel, the younger sister, was a shepherdess, while Leah, it is inferred, stayed at home, fulfilling the usual feminine role of the dutiful daughter. Rachel is described as being beautiful in form and appearance, while the best that could be said of Leah is that she had "delicate" or "weak" eyes.

Consider, however, the influence each of those vocations had on the girls. Rachel, being a shepherdess, likely lived an extremely active life, herding the sheep, soaking in the rays, kidding with the guys. Doubtless, as we are told nowadays, all the exercise was great for helping her keep and maintain that lovely form mentioned in Scripture. But being outside had an additional benefit: It kept the two sisters far from each other's throats. Leah, unlike her younger sister, led the traditional life of the daughter of the family, doubtless learning how to care for and feed the male members of the family. The problem about filling traditional roles, however, is that often a person gets taken for granted, especially if one is plain yet efficient in duty.

Thus, we see that the events that unfold in Genesis 29 didn't just "happen." All the seeds of rivalry and jealousy had already germinated, needing very little more for them to grow into nettles of pain. How long did it take for Leah to notice that her cute baby sister took all the limelight in a room? It doesn't take much to imagine how Leah's envy of her sister's beauty grew as, day by day, she seemed to fade into obscurity, while her sister, her spoiled and vivacious sister, charmed her brothers, her father—any of the male species who swam into her vicinity—with her smiles and chatter. What a relief it must have been for plain and practical Leah when Rachel's job took her outdoors day after day so that she no longer had to endure the slights of unfavorable comparisons between the two sisters.

Thus, an uneasy truce had been struck, since they barely saw each other. That is, until Cousin Jacob arrived on the scene. Rachel had all the luck, as usual, meeting their handsome and romantic cousin by the watering well. Out of nowhere he appeared, introducing himself as the son of Aunt Rebekah, who had ridden into the sunset to meet her Prince Charming so many years before. Quite possibly the two sisters had never met beautiful Aunt Rebekah, but it's guaranteed they would have drunk in with starry eyes the tales of the mysterious entourage that had swept away their aunt in a whirlwind of wealth and promises to meet her future spouse, a distant relative, sight unseen, with nevermore word from her—until Jacob arrived: her son! That alone lent him the mystique of being the lost link between two worlds, and for that he was gladly welcomed into the family, despite the fact that he had arrived with little more than the clothes on his back.

In fact, he would have been welcomed if he'd been an ugly, cross-eyed, knock-kneed weakling. It would have been better, in some ways, if he had been, because he wasn't ugly, not by a long shot. Scripture describes Jacob as being "smooth-skinned" (in contrast to his twin brother's hairiness) and strong (witness how he had single-handedly lifted the stone off the well's mouth). He was a man of contradictions: on the one hand mild mannered and gentle, able to cook, and familiar with the inner workings of a household (consequence of being his mother's favorite); yet on the other hand he was comfortable outdoors, a skilled worker with the livestock. One can see how this complex man must have appealed to each of the girls. Leah would have related well to Jacob's gentleness and his more "feminine" side, while Rachel would have appreciated his skill with the sheep. By the time Jacob had stayed with the family for a month, the stage was well set for the coals of the sisters' rivalry to be fanned into flames of jealousy and envy.

Of course, it was only to be expected that Cousin Jacob would fall in love with Rachel. Everyone did, for she was so beautiful. Yet perhaps Leah didn't despair, deeming it infatuation perhaps, even though Jacob was willing to work for seven years to earn Rachel's hand. Seven years is a long time in the eyes of young people; anything could happen.

But nothing happened. It was too bad, really. Jacob worked like a madman, dreaming of his love, seeing each year slide by as if they were nothing as he neared his goal. Rachel grew into womanhood, secure in her love, confident to wait, perhaps gloatingly so, for Leah was still there. Watching. Waiting. Wishing. One wonders why, in that space of time, Leah did not find a husband of her own. Was she that unlovely that no one would even look at her? Was she so unremarkable that no one noticed her practical presence as she cared for their daily comforts? Or had she been content to dream, hoping for some chink in the relationship, some miraculous event for her to get the man she dreamed of, longed for, day after day, as she mulled over the fact that *she* was perfect for Jacob, that *she* would be able to make him comfortable—not like that flitter bug of a beauty, Rachel.

Whatever the reason, Leah was still unwed at the end of Jacob's seven years of service, and when Jacob pressed the girls' father for his due wages, there she was, with no prospects on the horizon, hungry for romance and a family of her own. Maybe that's why Laban, the girls' father, decided to pull the switcheroo on Jacob when the bridegroom was drunk and meeting his bride in the anonymity of bridal clothes and darkness ... and maybe Leah didn't protest too hard, thinking to seize her only chance at happiness. All through that first night of loving, any niggling doubts were swept away in the passion of the moment, yet in that one act of deceit, she was deceived. Any chance of happiness and harmony between the three of them had been irrevocably shanghaied by their father's greed and Leah's dreams.

With the morning, Leah's castle of fantasy was humiliatingly and brutally shattered when her deception was revealed. Mild-mannered Jacob became a raving maniac: "'What is this you have done to me?'" Jacob roared to his father-in-law. "'Was it not for Rachel that I served you? Why then have you deceived me'" (Genesis 29:25)? Note that Leah is not even included in the interaction; it is as if she were nothing, an insignificant pawn, not worth any consideration. As her father stuttered about tradition and custom, trying to justify his actions, Leah's self-esteem was trampled in the rubbles of her shattered dreams. She got what she wanted for one week only, and when she felt her husband's rejection in the blast of his fury, her pulsating, pulverized heart must have whimpered in agony as his wrath was assuaged with Laban's promise that Jacob could wed Rachel too, after he did the obligatory wedding week with Leah. She got one week of physical relations, knowing that her husband only thought of her beautiful sister; one week, during which she desperately tried to stir up flames of love with the twigs of deception and deceit. And as she wept herself to sleep that night, the first of many such nights, did she regret the silly dreams and selfish desires that had conspired to blindside any positive relationship with her sister and Jacob?

That night of deception squelched any hope of harmony. Jacob and Rachel were one in love; Leah was the uneasy third cog. She was dutifully tolerated, for it was Rachel who Jacob yearned for and loved, while Leah desperately worked to earn his love, hoping that with each son God blessed her with, her husband would love her—just a little. Pitifully, Rachel was unhappy too, because her barrenness opened her up to the taunts of a hurting Leah. An ocean of unhappiness and a realm of hurt formed all because an unhealthy rivalry was permitted to fester into an open wound.

God was still able to work good out of such a scene of hurt, for out of that nasty situation a nation was conceived. But their story can apply well to our lives today. Their examples can be a caution sign, causing us to stop and re-evaluate our own lives and relationships. True, those sisters differed in many ways, with little drawing them together. Extreme differences in ages, in looks, in interests can drive siblings apart unless effort is taken to find a common ground. Unfortunately for Rachel and Leah, that common ground became Jacob.

Okay, bad common ground there, but it need not have festered into the situation it became. Essentially the burden of sacrifice would have fallen on Leah. Jacob had eyes only for Rachel. He worked hard for Rachel. He earned the right to marry Rachel. Rachel, Rachel, Rachel. It should have been obvious to Leah that there was no hope in that relationship. Therein was the problem. James 1:14, 15 says, "But each one is tempted when he is drawn away by his own desires and enticed. Then, when desire has conceived, it gives birth to sin; and sin, when it is full-grown, brings forth death." Leah had looked on Jacob. She was drawn into the idea of romance and given seven years to get out of the situation. For the sake of her relationship with her sister and for the possibility of peace in future years, Leah needed to get out of the situation, either by marrying someone else or by determining in her heart that she was not going to look upon Jacob as a possible spouse, deciding that he was untouchable to her. A sharp early hurt would have prevented the years of anguish and discord that the threesome endured for the years following that night of deception.

Practically, to heal sibling rivalry, effort must be taken to find common ground and interest that is neutral to both parties. Search for a common interest or cause to work on together, thus opening up the opportunity for communication and teamwork. Then, while working on that specific goal or task, focus on each other's strengths and put them to use. Learn to forgive, overlooking unintended slights and irritations as you strive toward a designated goal. If things get heated and tempers flare, take a break and give each other breathing space to recoup and simmer down. Romans 12:18 says, "If it is possible, as much as depends on you, live peaceably with all men." Do all that you can to keep the peace. Take care not to fan the embers of spitefulness and hurt pride that have been kindling in your life's hearth year by year.

Making the effort to lay aside jealousy and anger and choosing to mend fences and working toward peace and unity has to start with at least one of the rival siblings. It takes decided maturity on your part to choose to do so and will involve a lot of work. It may even ask that you make some sacrifices that hurt pretty bad, but making minor sacrifices now will prevent a world of heartache in future years. For a time, Leah and Rachel achieved a temporary peace by being separated as their respective occupations kept them apart, allowing each to develop her skills and ability in completely different fields, flowering in environments where they weren't being constantly compared to each other. Left at that, the two may have been fine if Jacob hadn't appeared on the scene. But since he did, and the situation worsened, drastic steps needed to be taken. There comes a time when someone has to decide to be willing to endure the pain of loving sacrifice, especially in a situation of conflict over a possession or person. Dreams and desires must be honestly evaluated in the light of love and Scripture: "Greater love has no one than this, than to lay down one's life for his friends"

(John 15:13). Sometimes healing only comes with self-sacrifice.

What do you need to do so that you won't have to live the rest of your life estranged from those who've been ordained to be your siblings? Choose the path of peace and togetherness, not the heartache and combat that so sadly characterized Leah and Rachel's relationship until Rachel's death.

Dinah

Genesis 34

> "Now Dinah ... went to see the
> daughters of the land ..."
>
> Genesis 34:1

"*If* only ..." Ever catch yourself agonizing, using those words? *If only I hadn't left everything to the last minute ... If only I hadn't treated that guy so badly ... If only I hadn't gotten drunk last night ... started smoking ... took up that dare ...* The list of regrets could be endless. Too often bad decisions are made, and the consequences spiral into such horrific proportions that you would give anything to undo that thoughtless action. You are not the only person who feels that way; Dinah, daughter of Jacob and Leah, after one thoughtless, impulsive outing, started a chain reaction of events that ended in a series of consequences that she must have regretted the rest of her life.

Dinah and her extensive family (she had twelve brothers, six of whom were full brothers) had just moved into Canaan. Genesis 33:18, 19 tell how her father, Jacob, had bought a plot of land adjacent to the city of Shechem on which to pitch the family tents. Perhaps missing the social life of her home in Haran, once they were all settled in and her brothers were out in the fields, minding their many herds of animals, Dinah decided to go and check out her new neighbors. The only girl in the family, she must have been hoping to make some new girlfriends, and the exotic sights and sounds tantalizingly drew her to explore. Such an innocent outing—or was it? Did Dinah stop to consider that new neighborhoods aren't necessarily safe and that perhaps she ought to wait and do the rounds with some of her family with her for protection? Did she even pause to consider that the culture and customs of this new land might vary from those her family followed? Evidently pretty, social butterfly Dinah had no second thoughts, and off she went to make some new friends.

Poor, thoughtless, innocent Dinah! Among those she met was Shechem, the spoiled prince of Shechem, after whom the city itself had been named (or was it the other way around?). What Shechem wanted, he took; he saw Dinah, wanted Dinah, and took Dinah—that is, he raped her. Perhaps customs were different there at that time, and it was usual for casual relations to occur outside the bond of marriage, because evidently having satisfied his lust, rather than cast her aside, Shechem's original attraction to Dinah became so strong that he decided that he wanted to keep her, to even marry her! He treated her kindly, carrying her to his home and installing her there, permanently, he hoped, as he then set about getting an official sanction from her family to marry her.

Dinah, not returning home that night, must have rung some loud warning bells in the minds of her parents, but when Jacob received concrete word of her rape, he chose to do nothing but waited for his sons to come home from the fields to break the news to them. That was a big mistake, because rumors have a nasty habit of flying quickly, and long before they were due to be home, Dinah's brothers heard what had happened way out where they had been working. The garbled version they heard was almost inevitably pretty graphic and coarse—perhaps a joke about how Prince Shechem had once again plucked an innocent girl off the streets to satisfy his personal lusts. When they realized it was their sister they were hearing about, the shock and grief was quickly eclipsed by volcanic anger erupting in their collective hearts. Vowing rescue and revenge, Dinah's brothers immediately deserted their posts and rushed home, revenge the driving emotion in their minds. In their minds, not only was their baby sister taken advantage of, violated, and made ineligible for marriage because she had lost her virginity, but they also perceived this act as an insult to their family honor. Simeon and Levi, two of Dinah's full brothers, were, in particular, completely incensed; to them this just wasn't something that was done, and there was no way they were going to let Shechem get away with this.

So enraged were they that Dinah's brothers seized upon Prince Shechem's honorable marriage proposal given by Shechem and his father, Hamor, as a tool for revenge, brushing away any chance of a peaceful resolution to the incident. Maybe what happened next wasn't their fault entirely, for the way Hamor set forth the request practically begged for them to do what they did next. Hamor didn't just ask that Dinah wed Shechem. No, he himself had seized upon the situation as a means to his own ends, putting forward the proposal in terms in which he suggested that this could be the start of a wonderful relationship between Jacob's family and the Shechemites. This, he said, was a great opportunity, a time of new beginnings, where all their sons and daughters could intermarry, and they'd all be one big happy family. Then trade between them would grow and their flocks would increase, with greater wealth to be gained and shared between them ... on and on he went. In short, he used the potential wedding between his son and Dinah as a means toward greater financial gain, making no mention of any love connection or consideration of Dinah's feelings in the matter.

Inwardly steaming, Jacob's sons hypocritically pretended that Hamor had a great idea, except for one itsy-bitsy problem: Neither Dinah nor any of their own daughters would be permitted to marry an uncircumcised man. Ignorant of Jewish customs or the reason why Jewish baby boys were circumcised, the pagan father and son had no clue about what circumcision really entailed, for in their alien culture, no one was ever circumcised. To their minds this qualification was something that could be quickly implemented, and once done, there would be no further barriers for intermarriage. Shechem, bedazzled by his new conquest, was so eager to wed that even had he considered the pain of such a procedure, he considered it a minor stumbling block in the way of his goal. Indeed, he was apparently eager to go through with the circumcision. Hamor, his father, was equally agreeable; no doubt visions of flocks, herds, and money danced through his head, dulling his senses to any possible scent of deceit. Their ignorance and blindness became their downfall.

Even as greed motivated Hamor, so it motivated his fellow citizens. When he presented to his people the benefits of absorbing this large family into their culture, the men agreed to submit to the procedure with little hesitation. Scripture tells us succinctly that in a remarkably short space of time, every male in that city was circumcised. Three days later, when the wounds were at the height of swelling and soreness and discomfort, Simeon and Levi, Dinah's full brothers, boldly swooped into and through the city, cold-bloodedly killing every one of those men, men who were too crippled with pain to defend themselves.

As if murder wasn't enough, the rest of the brothers also descended upon the hapless city, ostensibly to rescue Dinah, but in the process, they took the opportunity to completely plunder and sack it, carrying off not only the flocks, possessions, and wealth of the Shechemites, but also their wives and children. It seems only then was the brothers' thirst for revenge completely satisfied.

Personal violation and then a casual wipeout of an entire city—all of this occurred because Dinah had decided to go visiting on a whim. No other mention of Dinah is made in Scripture other than in family listings. It's as if when she disappeared back into the tents of her family, as a person she disappeared out of daily life. Living in retirement, did she continually retrace in her mind the events of that fateful day? Did the phrase "if only, if only, if only" run endlessly through her mind? One doesn't know, but the events of those few days must have been an awful lot to live with.

The story doesn't just stop there. The foreseeable result of this outrage perpetrated by the renegade brothers was that they had to move.

"What have you done?" their father ranted. "You have troubled me by making me obnoxious among the inhabitants of the land" (Genesis 34:30b). Instead of settling down and becoming absorbed into the Canaanite culture, they had to pull down the tents and hit the road again, mercifully protected by God, who instilled in the minds of the surrounding peoples a terror of God. Forfeiting the land he had just bought, Jacob, following God's directions, moved the clan toward Bethel.

Where was God throughout all of this? He was there all the time, for this was a time when he interceded repeatedly on behalf of the descendants of Abraham as he worked toward his goal of forging them into his own special people.

There is no way he could have instigated and condoned the deceit, anger, vengeance, and murder of Jacob's sons. Peppered throughout Scripture are God's strictures against those very sins. Time and again he says, "Vengeance is mine" (Deuteronomy 32:35). Knowing the hot tempers of mankind, years later God specifically instructed that people were to only extract an "eye-for-an-eye" (Exodus 21:24a) punishment when he also gave the Law to the expanded tribe of Israel. Thus he prevented any further mushrooming revenge such as what these brothers had visited upon the Shechemites. Yet when Dinah took her thoughtless, innocent walk and her brothers reacted to the results in ways that were definitely outside of his will, God used this black episode as a small puzzle piece, which, when combined with future events, produced an incredible picture.

Out of the shambles of this episode, God created something toward his ultimate glory, for if Jacob had been permitted to settle down and establish roots in that little plot of land outside of Shechem, within a short space of time he and his family would have been absorbed into the community, losing their identity as a people set apart for God. Now, because of this situation, God used the resultant isolation as a means to help them gain their own identity and reliance upon God, thus gradually becoming molded into the tribe that he had promised Abraham he would forge.

Dinah's thoughtless action was permitted to happen. After all, flitting off to go visiting was her own choice, but make no mistake, if she had been a little wiser, she would not have been hurt (nor Shechem and the males of his city killed, nor the city sacked), and God could have moved Jacob on using some other means. When looking back at the whole picture, it's easy to note how God took this horrible event and transformed it into a positive maneuver in the course of Israel's history, but there's no way Dinah could've seen that. For her that thoughtless walk was to reap years of remorse and regret, and that's a lot to live with.

It is not likely that a bad decision today would explode into the murder and sack of a city, but in individual lives, "small" poor decisions can mushroom into great personal destruction and the hurt of surrounding family and friends. It is even possible that a silly or stupid remark or act may be that little something that lights the fuse toward someone else's self-destruction or suicide, and the excuse "I didn't know" would be a poor comfort to your conscience. No one wants to live a life of regret, but what can one do?

Believe it or not, there is hope. Try for some wisdom and practical know-how. Where do you get that? Proverbs 1:7a says, "The fear of the Lord is the beginning of knowledge." Start with God. Realize that he created you, that he loves you, and that he sent his only son, Jesus Christ, to die on the cross for you, taking on himself your sins that separate you from the pure and righteous God and providing a way you can go to him personally. Acknowledge that you are a sinner, and take up the offer Jesus Christ provides. That is how you start. Once you are in God's family, then you have the help of the all-knowing and all-powerful God to help you pick your way through the pitfalls of life. Just ask!

The second step of learning to walk with wisdom and knowledge is to learn to follow the helpful hints and instructions God has given us. It's all written right there in the Bible. You have to read it, place it in your memory, and do what it says! Oftentimes God's instructions aren't popular to your friends (or you) because they don't ask you to do what everyone else does. Think of it this way: If God was personally involved in your creation and development (and he was—just check out Psalm 139), don't you think that he knows exactly what kind of guidelines you need so that you don't self-destruct in the murkiness of today's morals and temptations? It takes some work, but if you take the time to learn what not to do or how to do what pleases God as outlined in his Word, it is guaranteed that you will have far fewer regrets in your life than you would otherwise have.

Finally, knowing the ins and outs of God's standard isn't everything if you don't know how and when to put them into practice. Learn to take time to think things through before you make decisions, pause before your next hasty remark, and consider possible consequences—not from the point of view of what your friends think, but from what God would think (and remember, you can only know this if you are studying his Word to find out what he thinks!). You won't be perfect, but you won't be saying as many "if-only" phrases in your mind either.

What if, with the best of intentions, you mess up or you have messed up? What then? Remember this: You belong (or can belong) to a loving and merciful God. It is never too late to turn to him. Turn to him, pour out your troubles to him; he's always right there, ready for you. Learn that just as God worked in Dinah's day, so today he can use your situation to somehow, in his own inscrutable way, achieve good for his glory. Situations can be used to turn you back to him and to forge you in the crucible of hardship into a person whose character is more pleasing and more useful to him. At no time does he waste what you go through—if only because sometime in the future, after you have healed, he can use you to help someone else who is going through similar situations because you know where he or she is coming from. Turning to God is the only way you can heal and weather the consequences of your actions, confident in the knowledge that somehow God can use it for his own glory.

Don't be like Dinah, forced to live in the land of the "what-ifs" because she didn't think twice before she acted. Prevention is always the best tool; choose wisdom in the first place, but if you do mess up, turn to God and seek his forgiveness and help. As in Dinah's time, let him transform the "what-if" into something to his glory.

Jephthah's Daughter

Judges 11:29–40

"Do to me what has gone out of your mouth …"

Judges 11:36b

Jephthah's daughter: All her identity was wrapped up in that of her father's. There had always been the two of them, underscored as, year by year, her dad had bucked the stigma of being an illegitimate son in a respectable family in Gilead. Together the two of them had comforted each other during the hard times, laughing at hardship even as hunger sucked in their cheeks. Then, when her dad finally came into the big time, it was still just the two of them, but not for long.

She remembered how, as a child, she had listened avidly as he had told her of the time when his envious younger legitimate half brothers had chucked him out of the family as soon as their father had died. Spurned, driven out into the wilderness, penniless, and alone, those were the cutthroat years when Jephthah had learned to fight. Those were the years he had learned that he had the gift of leadership and was able to gradually mold the other worthless misfits who had ganged up with him into quite a fighting troop. Lean years, they were, but happy ones too, as she watched her beloved dad strive against the life he'd been tossed into. By the time she was on the threshold of womanhood, she knew without a doubt that her father had become a "mighty man of valor" (Judges 11:1b), whose fighting services were in great demand. She was so proud of him; how could she have known that in a very short time her hero dad would also be the instrument of her untimely death?

How thrilled Jephthah's daughter had been when the stigma of being illegitimate had been overshadowed by the tribe of Gilead's overwhelming need for her great warrior-dad and his elite troops to rescue them. In fact, the Gileadites, including his family, who had tossed him out in the first place (wow, that had felt good seeing them humbled before him), had begged him to lead them in their resistance movement against their oppressors, the Ammonites. They had even promised that if he won, he'd be given the leadership of the tribe. What a tantalizing idea, from pariah to head of the tribe! Now that was worth fighting for!

Thus one day Jephthah's daughter stood on their doorstep, seeing him off as he set his face toward victory and prestige. She was so proud of him; her dad was going to be the one to save Israel from those Ammonites who had dredged up an ancient grievance as a pretext of war,

Cameo Choices

seeking to carve out a wedge of Israelite land to add to their own lands. She knew he'd win, for wasn't he the best warrior of them all? In her mind there was no way he could lose, and already she was planning how she was going to celebrate his victorious homecoming.

When reading the progression of events as related in Judges 11, it's quite surprising how much this man Jephthah knew about his country's own history as he negotiated with the king of the Ammonites in the prelude to battle. Somehow, perhaps garnered in the early years in his father's household, Jephthah also knew of the God of Israel and how necessary it was to do it his way. Granted, he didn't know him too well (one has but to consider his lawless earlier life to realize this), but he did have the sense to commit the battle to God in Mizpah before setting out. That's when things got exciting. First, there were the talks, and then the rejection of terms by the king of Ammon, and then, wow! He could feel the Spirit of the Lord working in and through him. From that moment, everything went right. God had chosen to use him mightily, filling him with the Spirit of God so they could crush this people who had plagued Israel for so long. In verse 29 we find him filled with the Spirit, pursuing his enemies, zealous to free his people.

Yet as he and his troops started their advance and prepared to face the teeming hoards of the enemies, it suddenly became very apparent that even though Jephthah knew *of* God, was on the right path, and was being used by him, he still didn't *know* him very well. Perhaps it was the lust of battle or the testosterone rush of fight, but in an unwary, regretful moment, Jephthah tried to seal his victory by making an oath to God. This was totally unnecessary because Jephthah was already being enabled by God's Spirit to do marvelous things on the road to victory. Perhaps because of an unacknowledged, deep-seated insecurity from those years of rejection as a youth—whatever the reason—Jephthah felt he had to do one more thing to seal the deal for victory with God.

His mind on the chase, his heart yearning for victory and vindication, Jephthah opened up his mouth and uttered the first pious words that came to mind,

> "If You will indeed deliver the people of
> Ammon into my hands, then it will be that
> whatever comes out of the doors of my house
> to meet me when I return in peace from the
> people of Ammon, shall surely be the Lord's,
> and I will offer it up as a burnt offering."
>
> Judges 11:30b, 31

There the vow was; the words were out, and somehow his smattering of religion, his battle fever pitched white hot, and a slight remembrance of the home he was fighting for had gotten all mangled together in his mind. It sounded good. Obviously he wasn't thinking straight, however, for it doesn't seem possible that back home the livestock wandered at will through his home. The deed was done, however, and Jephthah promptly set the thought aside and started the advance.

Skip in your mind to his daughter at home, eagerly waiting for the news of the final outcome of the war that her hero-dad was leading. *What can I do to celebrate my dad's victory?* she wondered, never doubting for a moment that he wouldn't win. She loved to dance and sing and could play the timbrels; indeed, she loved to celebrate enthusiastically, given a plausible reason. *Well, isn't this a good excuse to give it my all?* she asked herself. She was sure that would please him. Didn't he love to watch her twirl and dance and sing as she flew at her chores? Ingrained in her memory was a tale of Israel's early history—how Miriam and the Israelites had sung and danced in celebration of God's deliverance of Israel at the Red Sea upon their escape from Egypt. What could be more fitting than to follow their example and, like them, lead a celebratory parade to greet her father when he returned victorious? So she made her plans and waited until at last she heard the news of victory and that he was almost home. As soon as the sound of his victory entourage could be heard in the distance, this hero's daughter, unable to contain her excitement, snatched up her timbrel and danced out to greet him, unwittingly unleashing her doom when she stepped out of her home.

Nothing happened as she had expected. For one thing, rather than grabbing her and twirling her around in excitement and with shouts of joy, as soon as he saw her, his face went dead white, and he stopped short, as if he'd been jerked back by a divine tether that had become too short. Flooding into his mind were those few hasty words he had sworn to God before battle: "If you will indeed deliver the people of Ammon into my hands … whatever comes out of the doors of my house … I will offer it up as a burnt offering" (Judges 11:30, 31). Victory dreams were shattered at his feet as the bile of self-disgust choked his throat.

Imagine her shock when her father, instead of greeting her with the love and affection with which he normally greeted her, "tore his clothes, and said, 'Alas, my daughter! You have brought me very low! You are among those who trouble me! For I have given my word to the Lord, and I cannot go back on it'" (Judges 11:35).

"Brought him low?" How could he say that to her? What had she done? Nothing—yet everything. How could she have known not to be the first one out of the door? She couldn't have, and now, because of his oath, her life was now forfeit. Then this teenage girl showed the true steel within her. Did she fight, argue, mouth out at him, or throw his words back at him? No, she did not.

> So she said to him, "My father, if you have given
> your word to the Lord, do to me according
> to what has gone out of your mouth, because
> the Lord has avenged you of your enemies,
> the people of Ammon … Let this thing be
> done for me: let me alone for two months,

> that I may go and wander on the mountains
> and bewail my virginity, my friends and I."
>
> Judges 11:36, 37

In other words, she asked for time to mourn and to come to terms with the fact that her life was being cut short and to adjust to the fact that she would never get the chance to marry and to hold a precious baby in her arms.

For two months she was in the mountains, two months of crying, possibly even screaming, in her heart to her God at the injustice of it all while she mourned with her friends. And then she went home to her death.

Not a happy ending, is it? How, one asks, could God allow such a thing to happen? Wasn't there anyone around to intercede for her, to say, "Hey, wait a minute, this is *wrong*"? Was there not one there who could point out the fact that yes, God had said that oaths needed to be carried out (Numbers 30:2), but of even greater importance was that God had forbidden the Israelites to burn their children as sacrifices like their heathen neighbors did for their false gods? No one stepped into the void, and she died.

Sure, she was mourned. Indeed, her friends remembered her sacrifice so faithfully that "it became a custom in Israel that the daughters of Israel went four days each year to lament the daughter of Jephthah the Gileadite" (Judges 11:39b, 40). In a sense God honored her for her obedience and sacrifice through this custom also because he inspired the author of Judges to include in the Scriptures this story about her.

Why is this story about Jephthah's daughter included in God's Word? Yes, Jephthah was one of the judges used by God to save his people when they so frequently were caught in the cycle of straying and then repenting of their sin when things got tough. It even makes sense that there needed to be a record of the events that led to the defeat of the Ammonites, but why include the story in so much detail, especially about a teenage girl? What lessons can be dredged from this mucky tale of woe?

The obvious first point is that we need to watch what we say and, more importantly, be careful about making bargains with God. He is the omnipotent God and knows what is best for us. In contrast, we are finite creatures who may end up regretting our sides of the bargains because we can't see far enough ahead. James 5:12 says, "But above all, my brethren, do not swear, either by heaven or by earth or with any other oath. But let your 'Yes' by 'Yes,' and your 'No,' 'No,' lest you fall into judgment." Using hindsight, Jephthah did fall into judgment. He lost his only child, thus ending his family line (something very important in Jewish society), but afterward God did not bless his judgeship. He only judged Israel for six years thereafter until his death, and those years were filled with strife, civil war, and slaughter.

Much more can be learned from Jephthah's daughter. She was definitely what we call a victim, helpless and powerless in a time when women had no life outside that defined by fathers or husbands.

Although a victim, this teenager showed a remarkable degree of self-control and maturity when confronted with sudden and devastating news of betrayal. This wasn't something minor. Her *dad*, the one who had loved her and protected her all her young life, was going to kill her. The safety she had felt in his arms no longer existed, and it was as if she were facing a stranger as she stared into his white countenance. In light of what she had just learned, it's remarkable what she did and didn't do.

In a situation where she could not undo the circumstance or the outcome, this remarkable girl chose to remain in control of her attitude and reactions. She didn't lose her temper. She didn't yell at him or argue or curse. Rather, she decided to interact with her father respectfully, daring to ask for a favor that did not reject his ultimatum, but which softened it somewhat, thus giving herself time to prepare herself mentally for what was ahead. As an adult and parent, this writer can tell you that when a parent delivers ultimatums, whether they are reasonable or not, if a teen chooses to react loudly against it, it is as if a match has been set against the fuse of a stick of dynamite; it makes a parent react even more strongly in that situation. Step back, defuse the situation with calmness, and give your parents some space. You'd be surprised how reasonable parents can often be if given some time to think things through when presented (later) with the appropriate facts.

Furthermore, not only did she speak respectfully to her father then; two months later she also obeyed him and returned from her outing to the hills, submitting to the fulfillment of his oath. Her dad had made a big mistake, yes, but in her eyes he was still her dad, and the love and respect she had grown up with enabled her to love him even then, even to the point where she gave up her life for him.

Another lesson to note is what this girl in crisis did *not* get: someone to intercede for her. As mentioned earlier, if just one person in authority had said to her dad, "Hey, wait a minute here. Let's study about what God really desires." If only one person would've stepped in between her and her dad in that moment of sacrifice, perhaps her story would have ended differently. Let the story of Jephthah's daughter clamor in your mind if it just so happens that you or anyone you know is facing abuse of any type; learn from Jephthah's daughter. Seek help, or it just might be too late.

Jephthah's daughter also shows us that in any situation where there is deep loss or injury, make sure you do what that teen did: Take the time to mourn, knowing that you may need not just minutes or hours or days, but even months. It's okay, even needful, to cry and shriek to God about what's happening. He's always there, listening, and he will hear your cry. Sometimes he does intercede in marvelous ways, but other times, like in this situation, he may not choose to change the course of events, enabling one to endure the situation instead. We see this by the very fact that after those two months of mourning, that girl did not run away or cause a huge stink. Rather, she chose to return to her father and face her fate—not an easy thing to do.

Didn't God care about what was happening to her? Yes. But why did he allow it to happen? That is a question that will have to be asked when we meet him face-to-face (if we're still wondering), but sometimes God allows situations to take place because he can see in the grand scheme of things how it will work out to his glory. The writer of Judges could not have known this, but if one explores the full compass of Scriptures, one notices something very interesting ...

It's almost like when a car whips past you, and you catch two or three notes to a song, but you can't quite identify it. The ideas of "father's oath," "innocent child sacrificed," and "save the people" sound so very familiar, but what do they remind one of? Then, suddenly the entire melodic line resounds in your mind's ear, and you remember the whole tune: "Wait a minute," you say to yourself, "it was similar to this song, but not quite accurate; for the real song really goes like this: 'Yes, there was a time, way back in the beginning, when there was an oath given, as set down for us in Genesis chapter three.'" Unlike Jephthah's reckless and unnecessary oath, however, this oath was uttered by the sovereign, omnipotent God, God the Father, as he fixed in place a just punishment for the serpent, Satan, thereby establishing the means for our redemption (see Genesis 3:14–15). Then, in the fullness of time, God the Father sent his only begotten son—not an innocent child like Jephthah's daughter, but one who was innocent of sin—into this world to be a sinless sacrifice for the penalty of our sins (John 3:16). Jesus, his son, did not deserve to die, even as Jephthah's daughter didn't, but unlike her in her powerless helplessness, he willingly "humbled Himself and became obedient to the point of death, even the death of the cross" (Philippians 2:8). Thus, he fulfilled the oath his father made so many, many years ago in our time frame. In such a way, we are subtly drawn to the cross through the story of Jephthah and his daughter. It's not a complete parallel; all it does is *remind* us of something and someone.

Thus, we see that the story of an innocent girl whose life was shattered by the reckless words of her father can teach us many things. She did not sacrifice her life for nothing. Her ordeal can teach us what to do in like crisis, but it also points us to the cross and to the one who can and will enable us to go through anything with him at our side.

Tamar

2 Samuel 13

"Do not force me …"

2 Samuel 13:12b

Tamar had everything—beauty, wealth, and status—for she was a princess, one of King David's daughters. But it was because of her beauty that she was destroyed, while her social standing in no way prevented the calamity.

Where there is great beauty, often there is great lust: That is the sad truth of this world. Tamar's oldest half brother, Amnon, noticed her great beauty, and Scripture says that he loved her to the point of illness. Whether it was love or lust, he wanted her at almost any cost. Amnon's cousin, Jonadab, noticed that he looked rather emaciated and asked what the problem was. Into his ear Amnon poured out his problem, and crafty Jonadab came up with a plan of deception for how Amnon could get his heart's desire.

"First pretend you're ill," he said. "Then, when the king comes to visit (Amnon was the firstborn son, King David's supposed heir to the kingdom, so this must have been a common occurrence), tell him that the only thing that will make you feel better is if your sister Tamar comes to your house and prepares a meal for you and feeds it to you."

Amnon followed Jonadab's instructions to the letter and suckered his father into delivering his sister into his clutches. Tamar had no idea that something was up. She knew that Amnon thought she was beautiful, but she also knew that she was a princess and a virgin. Thus, she was valuable to the family for possible key marriages. She'd heard that Amnon was ill, and perhaps she was a bit surprised that he wanted her cooking, but was there any reason for her to be suspicious? Her father had told her to attend her half brother, so she was simply being an obedient daughter.

At first there were plenty of servants and attendants around as she prepared the dinner. One wonders, however, if warning bells chimed in her head when he sent everyone out of the room but her. Then, when Amnon shifted the meal preparation into his bedroom, did she ask herself, *Why the bedroom?* Did she have any second thoughts, or was she so gullible and protected that she trusted her half brother so completely that she had no qualms about being alone with a man in his bedroom?

Once in the isolation of his own room, however, all was made clear as he grabbed her and said, "Come lie with me, my sister" (2 Samuel 13:11c). Scripture clearly records her objections:

> "No, my brother, do not force me, for no such thing should be done in Israel. Do not do this disgraceful thing! And I, where could I take my shame? And as for you, you would be like one of the fools in Israel. Now therefore, please speak to the king; for he will not withhold me from you."
>
> 2 Samuel 13:12, 13

Desperately, but in vain, she tried to point out the shamefulness of what he was planning. She pointed out what it would do to her. She told him that to do such a thing would make him a fool. She even offered an official way to the same thing: marriage. And even as she babbled, fighting for her purity, Amnon, blind and deaf to her pleas, proceeded to take his heart's desire. Read the description of a classic rape:

> However, he would not heed her voice; and being stronger than she, he forced her and lay with her. Then Amnon hated her exceedingly, so that the hatred with which he hated her was greater than the love with which he had loved her ...
>
> 2 Samuel 13:14, 15a

Afterward, having taken what he wanted and with his lust sated, Amnon callously dismissed her from his presence. Deceived, betrayed, raped, then abandoned by her attacker, Tamar resorted to the only thing left to her, passive resistance. She refused to budge from the room. Perhaps she hoped that someone would come upon them and force Amnon to be accountable for his actions. Maybe she thought that if she stayed long enough, he would eventually find the decency to "do the right thing by her" and make her an honest woman. Not so: Her half brother simply called his personal servant and had him forcibly eject her from the room. Humiliated beyond belief, with her violator's door slammed and bolted behind her, Tamar then ripped her beautiful many-colored robe, which had symbolized her chastity and status as a virgin princess. Throwing ashes over her head to illustrate her desolation, Tamar then staggered home, covering her face as she inconsolably wept over the physical and mental wounds she had sustained.

Absalom, her only full brother, found her in this state, and as she poured out her hurt and anguish to his questioning, little did she know that he was storing every tear of anguish in his heart, swearing to himself that somehow that half brother, that *worm* of a half brother, would be paid back in full (and more) for what he had done to his beautiful and precious sister. Although his words callously told her to forget about it and put it behind her, his actions acknowledged that such an act was impossible. Numbly she found that even as Amnon had spread himself over her and ripped one type of life from her, this brother spread his protection (belatedly as it was) over her by then taking her into his home, giving her a possibility of another sheltered life, where at least she would be hidden from the gossipers and lustful eyes of other men who thought that the spoiled goods might be available to them. There she remained desolate in his house, her bright and hopeful future now swapped for a life in the shadows. No marriage of any kind was ahead of her, let alone a royal alliance, for she was no longer a virgin. Physically attacked, stripped of dignity, bereft of purpose, what was left for her?

Amnon got what he wanted for the moment, but in the process he not only shattered his beautiful sister's life, but his own as well. In his monumental conceit, Amnon thought he'd gotten away with it because his dad, King David, although angry about it, didn't actually penalize him for the crime. The one thing he didn't take into account was that his younger brother Absolom loved his beautiful little sister, and he actually cared about what happened to her. He had no idea that even as his hand wasn't slapped for his misdemeanor, his brother Absolom was all the while nurturing the hate that had germinated in his heart the day he came upon the wreck of his sister weeping in the corridor. That hate he nursed day by day behind a front of indifference, adding any other insult or injury (including the fact that Amnon was the firstborn and first in line for the throne) until finally it festered into a plot of murder two years later. Through his plotting, Amnon was brutally murdered by Absolom's servants at a party Absolom had thrown for his brothers. Thus, he succeeded in not only avenging the wrong done to his sister, but at the same time, he moved himself one step closer to being heir to the throne. It is interesting to note, however, that even though Tamar's honor was supposedly avenged by Absolom, the only time when she is ever mentioned again is in the family genealogy; seemingly, when she disappeared into Absalom's house, she faded out of life.

Tamar's story shows two things. One, that rape, as we know, is a horrible thing. It violates every facet of a person's being—not only physically, but also mentally and emotionally. After being raped, it takes almost a miracle for a person to trust again. Shame and disgrace weigh the victim down, oppressing them into ineffectiveness and seclusion. Tamar's brother avenged her, but one would wish the Scriptures showed a path of healing and renewal for Tamar, for such is possible, especially through the healing wholeness Christ can work in the lives of those who trust in him. "Come to Me," he said, "all you who labor and are heavy laden, and I will give you rest. Take My yoke upon you and learn from Me, for I am gentle and lowly in heart, and you will find rest for your souls" (Matthew 11:28–29). Isaiah 53:4 says of Christ, "Surely He has borne our griefs and carried our sorrows." Indeed Jesus Christ, as God, knows what happened, he knows the pain of betrayal and suffering, and he knows your pain too. First Peter 5:7 says that you should be "casting all your care upon Him, for He cares for you."

Knowing that Christ loves you so much that he chose to die for you, don't hesitate; go straight to him, pour out your hurt, anger, sorrow, and bitterness, and set those cares into his loving hands. You will find that, indeed, Christ is still healing his loved ones today and that, somehow, your hurt will be transformed into something else. Additionally, if such a heinous thing should happen to you, also seek, as Tamar did, one whom you trust, tell what happened, and pursue justice. Never hide what occurred, for that path will never lead to complete healing.

The second lesson that can be learned from Tamar's life is how *not* to get caught in the situation that she did. Society worships beauty, styles seek to flatter it, and peer pressure takes advantage of it. First of all, don't fall into the trap of parading your looks and figure so that guys are given more of the opportunity to look and lust. Additionally, learn to use wisdom in the situations that you're in and figure out the signals for escaping before something bad happens. Consider Tamar. It was one thing to obey her father's command and bake the bread for her brother when Amnon's servants were around her as witnesses, but it was quite another thing when Amnon sent them all away. Note that one-on-one seclusion with another guy, however seemingly innocent it may be, potentially opens the door to problems. Again, when Amnon told her to come into his bedroom—whoa, run away, Tamar! Don't go there! One-on-one seclusion is suspicious enough, but going into a man's bedroom alone with him when you know that he admires you and wants you—that's asking for trouble. Choose the wise course. Don't go into a guy's bedroom alone with him. This sounds old-fashioned, I know, but lust is almost as old as this earth is, with the sex drive being particularly strong in certain situations. Even if rape doesn't happen, a lot of "stuff" could happen that you would regret after, particularly when it comes to the downward slide toward losing your purity.

Don't look at Tamar's story and say, "Oh, that's a terrible thing for Amnon to do," and then go away and forget all about it. Quite to the contrary, learn from her life and take heed, so that you do not have to go through what she went through. Money, social status, even a loving family cannot always buffer you from the sordid part of life, but you can take warning and be smart about whom you hang out with, where you go with any of the guys, and what you do with them. Use Tamar's story as a tale of caution; know that just as someone trusted—a family member—took advantage of a teenager back in the Old Testament Bible times, even today the same thing could happen to you or someone you know. Yes, you can trust, but don't be blindly trusting, either. If, like Tamar, your life has already been tainted and used by man's lusts and desires, take comfort. Here Scripture shows that someone else has gone through it and that you are not alone. God saw Tamar's grief and pain and did not ignore it. He sees yours too.

Abishag

1 Kings 1:1–4; 15

"And she cared for the king and served him …"

1 Kings 1:4

A decorative bed warmer is what they're describing, Abishag thought to herself as she digested the news with mixed disgust and alarm. Her thoughts jostled with the snippets of information that had been fed to her by the king's representatives. They had told her that she'd been selected out of the entire kingdom and that she was the loveliest of all the young unmarried virgins available throughout the entire land. They'd repeated over and over again that she was perfect for the job. They said that her services were vitally needed, gushing all the while that it was such an honor to serve the kingdom this way. And while the king's servants had bundled her and her possessions into the cart, barely allowing her time to bid farewell to her family and friends, Abishag had struggled to reconcile the two concepts in her mind: *How could being an old man's human heater be an honor?*

Initially, after being whirled away by those who'd chosen her, Abishag had found very little time to think through and get used to the idea of what her future would be. But since Abishag's home was in Northern Israel in Shunam, a little village smack dab in the middle of the small tribe of Issachar, it was a long, long way to their destination, her future home, Jerusalem. So, while they traversed the length of the Jordan River and then across Judah to Jerusalem, that lovely young lady had plenty of time to do just that: ponder, argue, and digest the multitude of conflicting thoughts that had been tumbling pell-mell through her head.

Running the gamut of homesickness to indignation at the haste of their departure ("King David is a very old man," the servants had said. "We mustn't waste any more time than necessary."), Abishag realized that it was pretty hard to build up any enthusiasm for the job at first. How could one get excited about having to care for the personal needs of a very old man and then a flesh-on-flesh warmer for his shaking torso? Here she'd been the prettiest girl in their village, courted right and left by the young men miles around. She'd been looking forward to a life of settling down as a wife and mother—eventually! At any rate, there's no way she could possibly have imagined that she'd dirty her pretty little hands and bed a palsied old man instead of a young, virile husband. From roaming a wide-open countryside, she was being condemned to service in a few well-appointed and richly furnished rooms for who knows how long. And then, well, what would happen after the king died? Would there be any future after her time of service? What status would she have then? What would people think?

One thing was obvious to Abishag: This service she was to provide certainly put to death any typical ideas of romance, courtship, and marriage! With the early dreams she had nurtured about her future firmly squelched by the reality into which she was being plunged, Tamar found that it was suddenly necessary for her to rearrange her expectations about what her future might mean.

Having settled that issue in her mind, Abishag then started actually thinking about the person to whom she was to be devoted. The only king she had ever known about in her young life was King David. By now he had been Israel's king for almost forty years. True, she'd never actually seen him, as by the time she'd been born he was getting to be quite old and settled in his capital city of Jerusalem, but hadn't she grown up with the stories about all his mighty fights and incredible victories? Her own grandmother had repeated again and again the stories of the times when she and her girlfriends had danced and chanted, "Saul has slain his thousands, and David his ten thousands" (1 Samuel 18:7b), chuckling all the while as she related his various exploits.

To her grandmother, King David had been a hero to sigh over. To her mother, King David had been an active conqueror, just and zealous for his country, but also a hero with feet of clay. Many were the times she'd clucked over the problems that troubled King David's family life, all the while remarking that even with his problems, King David's faith and love of their God was a beacon and example for his people to follow. "Look at his songs," Abishag's mother would say. "His heart and soul are laid bare to anyone who cares to listen. Every single one shows us something about his relationship with our God. Listen close and you'll see how much he loves him …"

Yes, Abishag said to herself, *King David really does love our God in a way I can only imagine … and look at the stability of this nation, and all because of the many battles our king fought to expand and protect our borders!* The more she thought about it, the more Abishag realized that she—country-bred, little miss nobody—she, Abishag the Shunammite, was actually going to meet this warrior king in person! She was going to be caring for a *legend!* And so disgust and disappointment gradually gave way to a reluctant realization of the honor conferred on her in being chosen to care for their aging king. When, after a long and tiring journey, as she and her escort entered the city of Jerusalem and pulled up to the palace, Abishag was finally ready and willing to serve as she nervously prepared for her imagined vision of King David to be displaced by reality.

If you read 1 Kings 1:1–4, you will note that much of the above mental dialog I just wrote is purely from my imagination. Perhaps Abishag simply went to serve the king without question, deeming it a duty. This author chooses to think that she was a typical teen with warring emotions, secret ambitions and a vivid imagination. For a very beautiful young teen to be told to care for and warm an elderly man, even if he *is* The King, isn't a natural thing to be willing to do—or at least the idea would be considered with serious misgivings.

What we do know about Abishag the Shunammite is that "the young woman was very lovely; and she cared for the king, and served him; but the king did not know her" (1 Kings 4:4). In verse 2, we learn that her primary job was to "let her stand before the king, and let her care for him; and let her lie in your bosom, that our lord the king may be warm." In other words, she was to care for his physical needs, which included washing, toiletries, and flesh-to-flesh, side-by-side cuddling to warm him up as he shivered night by night under the blankets. Scripture is very careful to mention that this was not a sexual relationship, but a relationship of necessity, one where she was so close to him that in all aspects she was a wife to him except for the sexual union. It would not have been easy, dealing with the incontinence that so often demeans the elderly, or enduring the brittle bones that pressed into her flesh, bones covered with withered sinews and wrinkled skin that defied any attempts on her part to imagine what he might have been like as a young man. It must have saddened Abishag as she witnessed the lapses of memory or any of those other indignities that plague the aging body of man, yet day by day and night by night, she faithfully cared for his every need, always standing by his side.

Toward the end of King David's life, when his son Adonijah tried to supplant the heir Solomon and worm himself onto the throne, Bathsheeba, who was one of his wives, sought an audience with him to try to head off the incident. Who should be attending him at the time? Abishag, always there, installed so securely that King David's wife didn't even raise an eyebrow at her presence.

Such a job did have a consequence however. Because of her extreme closeness to King David, even though she was not a wife or concubine in reality, the intimacies of service placed her technically in the position of "honorary wife," as it were. We know this, because after Solomon was crowned king and Adonijah's plans were foiled, Adonijah tried one more time to usurp the throne, using Abishag as a front. After King David died, he pretended that all he wanted was to marry Abishag, yet when the proposal was set before wise King Solomon, Solomon hit the roof: "Now why do you ask Abishag the Shunammite for Adonijah? Ask for him the kingdom also—for he is my older brother—for him, and for Abiathar the priest, and for Joab the son of Zeruiah!" (1 Kings 2:22b) Because Abishag had been so close to King David at the end of his life, her implied status as honorary wife was strong enough to trick Adonijah into thinking that if he married her, he'd be marrying the king's wife and thus would gain status and precedence over Solomon, his younger brother. King Solomon knew that if Adonijah was thinking that, others were probably willing to go along with him on it, and if he permitted the marriage, he would be hazarding his future as Israel's king. Plotted treason violated

Adonijah's probation, and he was executed immediately. Thus, Abishag's only marriage proposal came about because of some slinky court intrigue.

In essence, when Abishag went into service for King David, she became completely devoted and set apart for his use and needs. In one sense she became a holy person, because she was completely set apart for him and him only, for always. Even after his death, she was still untouchable.

This aspect of being set apart, of complete and devoted service to the king, is what appeals about the story of Abishag. Whatever her previous thoughts and misgivings might have been, by the time she got to the King, she was a devoted and satisfactory servant to her master, willing to meet his every need. Consider yourself as an Abishag. In this day and age you will never be told to be a servant and body-warmer to a king (not only because there's a general lack of kings around, but also there are much better tools for adding body warmth to chilled bodies), but in a spiritual sense we are all Abishags.

Every one of us is asked to serve the King of Kings. When King Solomon had first been crowned as king, God had said to him, "As for you, my son Solomon, know the God of your father, and serve him with a loyal heart and with a willing mind; for the Lord searches all hearts and understands all the intents of the thoughts" (1 Chronicles 28:9).

Hundreds of years later, the prophet Isaiah was given a promise by God (the same God who called David and his son Solomon to his service) that "also the sons of the foreigner Who join themselves to the Lord, to serve him, and to love the name of the Lord, to be His servants … Even them I will bring to My holy mountain" (Isaiah 56:6a, 7a). We are called to come to him, to love him, to serve him!

The apostle Paul continues the concept of our service to God: "I beseech you therefore, brethren, by the mercies of God, that you present your bodies a living sacrifice, holy, acceptable to God, which is your reasonable service" (Romans 12:1). Have you chosen to answer that call and enter into that service? One where, like Abishag, you will be set apart entirely for his service, willing to do whatever is asked, doing it well, and being wholly his? Let the cry of your heart be even as David expressed it, "Teach me to do Your will, for you are my God" (Psalm 143:10a). "'Behold,' God says, 'I stand at the door and knock. If anyone hears My voice and opens the door, I will come in to him and dine with him, and he with Me'" (Revelation 3:20). You are called. Will you answer and serve?

Naaman's Captive Girl

2 Kings 5

"Thus and thus said the girl who
is from the land of Israel."

2 Kings 5:4b

She was plucked from her home and family like a cherry stolen by ravenous blackbirds. No warning and no good-byes. Stolen in a lightning-quick raid by Syrian elite troops, our heroine then became a slave to the wife of her captor. With her life spinning out of control into one she could not call her own, this girl chose to do more than survive. Like a stone thrown into still waters, her actions sent ever-increasing ripples into her world, impacting her master's life richly, influencing Syria and Israel in ways she never could have imagined, and enriching her own life far beyond mere servitude.

How did this all happen? How could the God of her

nation have permitted this? It all had a lot to do with the times and events into which this girl was born. The glory days of King Solomon were a distant memory. Present reality was a kingdom torn into two nations, Israel and Judah. Like the days of the judges (the pre-king era of Israel), the divided nations wallowed in bouts of faithlessness, intermingled with occasional shining years of faithfulness to the God of their fathers. According to 2 Kings 3:1a-2, this was a time of poor spiritual health with Israel being led by King Jehoram, a man who only cried out to God when things got tough. Consequently, Israel was constantly hassled by bordering countries, namely Moab and Syria, as permitted by God's punitive displeasure.

Syria's king was Ben-Hadad (2 Kings 8:7), whose army commander, Naaman, had been ably terrorizing Israel by unleashing lightning raids across her borders. These raiders would swoop in and snatch not only animals and possessions, but also people as possessions. Our heroine was one such victim. She is given no name in Scripture, other than "young girl," revealing that she was older than suckled babe but younger than mature maidenhood.

A victim, yes. Victimized? No. Second Kings 5:2 encapsulates this girl's progression from free Israelite, to terrified captive, to trusted servant girl—trusted to the extent that she was personal servant to the high commander's wife.

Not only was she a servant in position, however, but she also served wholeheartedly, taking a personal interest in the cares and woes of her masters. Indeed, those woes were heavy. For Naaman, favored commander of the

Syrian Army, had contracted an incurable, pariah-making disease: leprosy. Akin to the scourge of AIDS in our society today, a person in that day and age usually became an outcast, shunned by society, isolated from family and friends. It was an ironic situation, really; just as our girl's life had been turned upside down, so her captor's life was careening out of control.

Rather than gloat, however, this heroine, in concern, wistfully murmured to her mistress a memory of something from her pre-captive days: "If only my master were with the prophet who is in Samaria! For he would heal him of his leprosy" (2 Kings 5:3). This whispered yearning in her mistress's ear became transposed into a thin possibility passed on by a consoling wife to her ailing husband. With no other possibility of relief in sight, Naaman desperately seized this tiny thread of hope spun by the tale of his captive Israelite servant and ran with it.

The rest is history, as recorded in 2 Kings 5. With his king's blessing, Naaman sought out the prophet Elisha, was instructed by the prophet to dip seven times in the Jordan River, and was healed (after being persuaded by his servants to fully obey the instructions given). A grateful man, whole physically and spiritually, Naaman then returned home with soil from Israel on which to worship the only true God (2 Kings 5:15a, 17).

One girl's word brought about her master's healing; one girl's testimony helped her master learn of the one true God. Therein she would have been content. But even as the laws of nature demand that the impact of a stone in still waters must have a reaction, so her concern and bold speech rippled in tantalizing heaves across the fabric of her two countries.

Reading farther in Scripture, 2 Kings 6:8–12 relates a knotty predicament of the Syrian king, Ben-Hadad. This was a time when all his plots against Israel had been foiled again and again by an unknown agent. Seeking a spy in the midst of his servants, one of them said that the problem was not with them but that "Elisha, the prophet who is in Israel, tells the king of Israel the words you speak in your bedroom" (2 Kings 6:12). It cannot be proved that it was Naaman who spoke up, but he *was* a favored companion of Ben-Hadad (see 2 Kings 5:1, 18), and he personally knew of Elisha as God's tool, so it is a possibility. King Ben-Hadad, in reaction to the information, then tried to capture Elisha but ended up with his own troops captured instead. Ultimately, after the captured troops were treated kindly, feasted, and sent home, 2 Kings 6:23b says, "So the bands of Syrian raiders came no more into the land of Israel."

Could it be that the kind testimony of a captive Israelite girl indirectly brought about a time of unexpected peace? Be that as it may, at the very least, her master had been healed of a devastating disease and brought into a relationship with her God; that in itself would have been satisfactory enough.

But what can this girl and her choices in that specific crisis of her life teach us today? How did she achieve balance amidst turmoil? The anchor, first and foremost, in this captive girl's life was that she knew what she believed. In a time of a spiritual slump, this girl still somehow knew of the God of her nation and of the powerful prophet who was his mouthpiece. Have you been thrown into a tailspin by a series of unforeseen events? Have the winds of circumstance whipped the umbrella of your life inside out with parental job loss, sudden transfers in work resulting in abrupt moves, or divorces resulting in constant jockeying between bitter parents? What about natural disasters, like the flooding of New Orleans or when a tornado wipes out your whole town? In situations like this, where there is absolutely nothing you can do to change what happened, how do you hang on and not lose your self control? What about so-called smaller things, like a fight with your best friend or the death of someone you love?

Know this: If you are solid in your relationship with Christ and you know what you believe in times of calm, then in the midst of the storm you will be strong and able to stand. Scripture says, "Therefore take up the whole armor of God, that you may be able to withstand in the evil day, and having done all, to stand" (Ephesians 6:13). The "evil day" mentioned in this verse could be anything that shakes you up so bad that you could potentially become insecure in your trust and faith in God. In context, taking up the armor of God is related to being prepared in your spiritual walk for spiritual warfare. But being prepared and "taking up" all has to do with your walk with God. Spiritual warfare walks in tandem with disastrous events in our lives, practically speaking. Be prepared, and thus stand.

A further stabilization for the servant girl was the result of having an acquiescent spirit, hand-in-hand with a good attitude. Rather than becoming embittered, angry, and sullen, this Israelite captive chose to accept the situation, learn from it, and do her best within it. She could have gloated over her master's misfortune, but she empathized instead, mourning that he couldn't see the great prophet. Choosing to tint the situation through the glasses of a right attitude pushed this young girl past her own misfortune and into the lives of those who surrounded her in her new life. If the decision had been made to sulk and turn inward, only doing what was demanded of her, this girl's master would never have been healed. But she noticed the distress of her mistress and master and dared to speak up. Heaven only knows what the downward spiral might have been if she hadn't spoken; we know from Scripture the good that came from choosing to get involved.

A young captive girl from Israel she became; a captive girl she remained. Yet despite the situation, this young lady chose to remain strong rather than crumbling under the distress. The choice was hers, and she chose to go on with life. What would you choose?

Esther

> "She requested nothing but
> what Hegai … advised."
>
> Esther 2:15b

Myrtle. That's what Hadassah means. Something nice and ordinary, a safe Jewish name. But that was the problem: There was nothing ordinary or safe about this Jewish girl. There was no way this third-generation captive in Babylon could hide in the woodwork and pass unnoticed. Some people might consider it a blessing, but being outstandingly lovely wasn't necessarily a good thing if you didn't want to be noticed. That may have been why Hadassah was given the Persian name of Esther, meaning "star," for her loveliness made her shine in the neighborhood whether she liked it or not. No one had any idea that her Persian name was to be a prophetic one.

Indeed, for a time Esther might even have cursed in her heart that she was so incredibly beautiful.

Up to the time of this story, life had not been easy for Esther. She was a captive and a descendant of captives, an exile in an alien land. She and her people had no rights and nothing in common with the melting pot culture of the Persian Empire. All her young life, her heritage meant possible persecution or scorn; indeed, the goal of most Jews at the time was to pass unnoticed and unremarked by the people of the land in which they lived so uneasily.

In addition to her lowly status, Esther was also an orphan. Thank God that her older cousin Mordecai had been willing to be her guardian. Scripture does not say how young Esther was when her parents died, but it's obvious that there was great affection between these two. Esther had learned early to honor and respect this politically savvy cousin of hers, being willing to abide by his wisdom in everything.

At this time King Ahasuerus of the Persian Empire was having marital difficulties, and in the end he divorced his wife, Vashti, removing her from the position of queen. Politics weighed in here as much as anything else, and she had been put aside because of her bad example of disobedience to the "noble ladies of Persia and Media" (Esther 1:18a). That didn't stop the king from missing having a queen after his temper cooled and he had the leisure to think about what had happened, so his counselors proposed that he find a new wife. The plan they placed before King Ahasuerus for finding a new queen was that all the beautiful young virgins in his kingdom were to be gathered willy-nilly, whether they wanted to or not, like exotic birds of paradise, and given extensive beauty treatments. After the mandatory twelve months of preparation, each girl was then given one night to be presented to the king, afterwards becoming one of his concubines if not chosen to be queen. With King Ahasuerus's approval, the search was instituted, and soon the beautiful young star of her neighborhood, Esther, was caught in the net.

Poor Esther. One wonders what must have been whirling through her head. Was she questioning God in her heart as to why he had to make her beautiful? Surely she was thinking that it would have been better to be plain and ugly and home with her family, safe in anonymity, than to be forcibly hauled off and immersed in pagan Persian culture, which was bad enough. Far worse, she was to be compelled to try to please the king for one night, most likely to be cast off as his concubine and live the rest of her life shut up in the house of women! Consider, too, how every Jewish girl's goal was marriage and motherhood, of being the mother of the coming Messiah. Now any such option was wrenched from her grasp. Given this situation, anyone, let alone Esther, would have questioned how God could have allowed this to happen.

In addition to her world being turned topsy-turvy, as she was being hustled away, her cousin Mordecai added to her alienation by hastily commanding her to keep quiet her ethnicity and family. Of course, she knew this would help her fit in better, allowing her to make her own way without the stigma of being one of those Jewish captives, but that also meant she had to be willing to participate in much that would have appalled her God-fearing compatriots, including eating many foods they wouldn't even touch.

By forswearing her heritage, was she forswearing her God too? Her relationship with her cousin was to be severely limited now and any connection with those of her heritage completely severed. That was a tough transition to make. Eve rything was to be different for her: her relationship, culture status, and future. Nothing was ever going to be the same again for this sweet, sheltered Jewish girl.

If she was questioning God and his control of the circumstances of her life, soon Esther's fears were temporarily allayed. Immediately upon arrival at the king's palace, Hegai, the eunuch in charge of the whole process and the one responsible for the girls' preparations, immediately took a fancy to her. Before she knew it, the bewildered girl found herself in the best suite of the women's quarters with seven extremely competent maidservants with all her needs met and preferential beauty treatments given to her.

Thus, she was enrolled in the prescribed yearlong beauty course, which was the prelude of a changed life and lifestyle. Month by month, she first bathed daily in oil of myrrh for six months and then endured six months of perfume treatments and other beauty preparations that erased any possible flaw or imperfection of skin and complexion. Day by day, her cousin Mordecai paced in front of the court of the women's quarters, hoping to get some news about her. Hour by hour, time relentlessly paced closer to that fateful moment when she was to go in to the king. Time, whether it crawled by because of the sheer tedium of the same old routine of beauty treatments or whether it raced by relentlessly, dragging her toward the night that everything was devoted to, finally seemed to stop when at last it was her turn to visit the king.

It helped that Hegai still looked out for her. In fact, she'd come to respect his experience and practical wisdom, so when it was her turn to be taken in to the king, she asked his advice about what she needed to take with her before entering the king's presence. Perhaps being well prepared made her more comfortable in the situation, enabling her to be her own sweet self, for she certainly made an impact on King Ahasuerus that night. Miracle of miracles, the king loved her "more than all the other women, and she obtained grace and favor in his sight more than all the virgins; so he set the royal crown upon her head and made her queen instead of Vashti" (Esther 2:17). Thus, Esther went into the king's presence a beautiful, unknown maiden and departed as queen, the new rising star in the kingdom.

Becoming the new queen certainly was more than she could have hoped for, but it wasn't until nearly nine years after being crowned that it became obvious to her why God had allowed her to be thrust into such a position. Her position as queen then enabled her to intervene and save her people, from the certain annihilation plotted by the evil plotting of Haman, the king's second in command.

Nine years is a long time to wait for answers. When torn

from the only family she knew, how did Esther flourish instead of crumble in the face of this apparent disaster? What enabled her to adjust to this foreign path that ran directly counter to anything her Jewish upbringing would have prepared her for? How was she able to remain beautiful inside and out, rather than becoming angry and bitter as year by year she languished in the king's harem, queen in name but still uncertain of the king's favor and attention, knowing her life to be on a tiny thread, easily snipped if the king was to lose his temper? What enabled her to retain her stability, sanity, and faith in God? Think about Esther's character, her personal background, and how she interacted with those around her, and one begins to understand how she refrained from being a fallen star but rather soared to the heights in the situation she was thrown into.

Esther's first and obvious characteristic is that she had a very stable personal identity. Although an orphan, she had very strong connections with her people, the Jews. Even though she had to sever any contact with those very people, she still knew who she was and retained a deep love for them, remembering always that they were God's own special people. Thus, when thrown into an alien society, she still had a steady personal identity and faith that served as bedrock to her soul. It also gave her a purpose, enabling her to lay her life on the line in order to save her people. "If I perish, I perish" (Esther 4:16c), she had said to her cousin Mordecai. Knowing who she was and where she came from thus provided Esther with a strong anchor in trying circumstances.

Another aspect that helped Esther was that her beauty

was not solely superficial. Esther 2:7 describes Esther as being both lovely and beautiful in an attempt to point out the multifaceted depth of her beauty. Far more telling is the fact that she pleased Hegai, under whose custody she had been placed, not just at the time of first impressions, but even more so at the end of the twelve months of beauty preparations. Not only was she still in Hegai's favor, but she also "obtained favor in the sight of all who saw her" (Esther 2:15d).

This beauty is first seen in her strength of character when she chose to submit to Mordecai's advice and command when he told her not to tell anyone of her heritage. Later she also chose to submit to Hegai, humbly seeking his advice when it came time for her to go into the king instead of doing what she wanted to do.

In addition to strength of character, inward beauty was shown by the fact that she wasn't greedy or selfish. It was the custom, when preparing to go to the king, that each girl was permitted to take anything that she desired with her; such possessions going with her, of course, when she was transferred from the place of the virgins into the king's wives' and concubine's quarters. In contrast to tradition, Esther showed her unselfishness when she "requested nothing but what Hegai the king's eunuch, the custodian of the women, advised" (Esther 2:15b). Her quiet restraint and humility thus highlighted and augmented Esther's extraordinary external beauty.

This relationship with Hegai the eunuch and Mordecai underscored another characteristic of Esther's that is all-important: She respected authority. She illustrated this when she obeyed Mordecai about not revealing who she was and then later when Mordecai commanded her to step in and save her people. When she obeyed Hegai and sought his advice, an attitude of respect was obvious. plus, it was seen when she took seriously every command her king gave. Even when he showed favor to her, she still showed respect in every word and action, beyond the call of duty.

Early in Esther's life, she had learned the importance of obeying the authority that was placed above her; thus, when she was flung into the silken court of Persia, she made sure that she aligned herself properly with authority. Because of her attitude and habit of submission, her personal appeal grew in the eyes of those in authority, ultimately protecting and aiding Esther far beyond what she could have accomplished on her own.

Additionally, when thrown into a difficult situation, Esther made the best of it and submitted to the unfolding events. In other words, she had a good attitude. She did not sulk and throw temper tantrums, or attempt to escape somehow, or grow bitter—all attributes that would have soured her quickly in the eyes of Hegai. Rather, she chose to submit her will toward acting in a positive manner, behavior that quickly placed her in comfort and favor during the preparation time. Attitude dictates how one perceives and responds to tests and trials; Esther's attitude enabled her not only to submit to what she was going through, but also to grow and improve, in short, to flourish dramatically.

The final all-important aspect in Esther's life that

helped her through every twist and turn was that she had a deep and abiding faith in God. It is surprising that the Book of Esther never once mentions the name of God. Neither does it say that she spent time praying like the earlier Jewish patriots Daniel, Hananiah, Mishael, and Azariah (Daniel 2:17–18). To make this claim about her beliefs is to realize two things: one, the belief that they, the Jews, are God's chosen people is the very core component of their national identity; two, when her guardian, Mordecai, pushed her hard and told her that she had to stick her neck out for her people, Esther sent the following message back to him: "Gather all the Jews who are present in Sushan, and fast for me; neither eat nor drink for three days, night or day. My maids and I will fast likewise" (Esther 4:16b). Look it up, and you'll find that fasting is part of petitioning God Almighty. When times were critical, Esther indeed knew to whom she needed to turn.

Ours is a society of transience; increasingly, it has become less common for a person to grow up and remain in the same town or even family that one is born into, whether because of job changes, split family, or chasing the elusive dream of happiness. Moving isn't easy. Facing stressful situations can cause a person's life to spin seemingly out of control. How can a teen placed in such a situation retain her sanity? Is it possible to flourish when transplanted with or without her consent? Today it is highly unlikely that any young and beautiful teenage girl would be cast into such a role as Esther played, but there are times when people are abruptly pushed into situations that spell certain unwanted changes in their lives and lifestyles, instances where they are helplessly out of control. Let Esther's life and example show you how it's possible to go far beyond simple endurance and yearning to escape whatever you've been haplessly thrown into.

First of all, what is your personal identity? Do you know who you are and where you're going? Great stability could be yours as a child of God. The apostle Paul suffered a great deal for the sake of the cross, but he never wavered in his faith, saying to his pupil, Timothy, "For this reason I also suffer these things; nevertheless I am not ashamed, for I know whom I have believed and am persuaded that He is able to keep what I have committed to him until that Day" (2 Timothy 1:12). One of the bedrocks of His faith was his supreme confidence in the love God had for him:

> "Who shall separate us from the love of Christ?
> Shall tribulation, or distress, or persecution,
> or famine, or nakedness, or peril, or sword?
> … For I am persuaded that neither death nor
> life, nor angels nor principalities nor powers,
> nor things present nor things to come, nor
> height nor depth, nor any other created thing,
> shall be able to separate us from the love of
> God which is in Christ Jesus our Lord."
>
> Romans 8:35, 38–39

Are you a child of God, privileged to know that you are in the care of your Father because of the sacrifice his only begotten son was willing to undergo for you? As a child of God, have you spent time daily in his Word, getting to know him better, learning what he expects of you, and claiming the many promises he has given? Have you determined in your heart to love, serve, and please and obey him? Psalm 34:8 says, "Oh, taste and see that the Lord is good; Blessed is the man who trusts in Him!" Take that step, put your trust in him, cement your identity with his, and no matter what you go through, you can remain stable.

Having established how to become anchored first of all, the next thing you need to evaluate about yourself is, how beautiful are you? I'm not talking about external beauty here, but all the ingredients that make up a person of quality and good character, that inward beauty that is so appealing to God and others around you. Esther showed the beautiful characteristics of humility, unselfishness, respect for authority, and a positive attitude in the crisis she went through. If you were thrown into a trying situation, what would come popping up to the surface when you weren't looking? Scripture is filled with hints and commands about traits that should characterize a child of God.

As a starting point, do you love others? First John 3:23 says, "And this is His commandment: that we should believe on the name of His Son Jesus Christ and love one another …" Earlier, in chapter 3 verse 16, the author said, "By this we know love, because He laid down His life for us. And we also ought to lay down our lives for the brethren." Then verse 18 finishes off the thought: "My little children, let us not love in word or in tongue, but in deed and truth." Much more could be said about this topic, but learning to love others, whether they deserve it or not, is one of the main characteristics that should distinguish a child of God.

Adding to this precious basis of love, the apostle Peter gives us some sage advice aimed specifically to our gender:

> Do not let your adornment be merely
> outward—arranging the hair, wearing gold,
> or putting on fine apparel—rather, let it be
> the hidden person of the heart, with the
> incorruptible beauty of a gentle and quiet spirit,
> which is very precious in the sight of God.
>
> 1 Peter 3:3–4

Part of Esther's great beauty that was so compelling to King Ahasuerus was this "hidden person of the heart." All the other girls had gone through the same year's beauty course that Esther went through, yet there was something special about her. Take this verse to heart and seek clues from Scripture about how to gain inner beauty, all the while not forgetting to ask God for his help in this area. As you work to please God, you just might start discovering that gradually you are becoming more like Esther, who "obtained favor in the sight of all who saw her" (Esther 2:15d), which, in the long run, makes things a whole lot better, no matter what you go through.

Finally, part of Esther's appeal, strength, and stability came from the fact that she respected authority and had no problem with humbling herself and submitting to the various people she was placed under: first, Mordecai, her cousin, then Hegai, the eunuch, then King Ahasuerus. Note that obeying her cousin might have been easy because there was a strong bond between them, but there was no such basis between her and Hegai or King Ahasuerus. With them she had to simply determine in her heart that they were the bosses. Thus, she needed to respect and honor them in their positions. The determination came first; the mutual liking and respect only came afterwards. Take warning though: The good that happened to Esther is not guaranteed to happen in your situation, but treating those in authority over you—parents, teachers, your boss at work, and so on—with respect and honoring their authority will stand you in good stead wherever you go and whatever you do. Guaranteed.

It is completely possible for you to be suddenly uprooted and torn from the very familiar and all of your friends if your parents have to move, isn't it? Sometimes moves aren't just into a similar neighborhood, but sometimes into another land, culture, or any situation when you become the minority instead of the majority. What is your attitude? Are you willing to submit to authority? Are you willing to work in the situation so that you grow more beautiful inwardly, triumphing in such a way that you are in favor with both parents and others around you?

Being a Christian, what if you are plunged into a

situation where you have to stand for your beliefs and risk total humiliation? Are you established and so solidly set in your identity as a child of God that you are willing to risk all for him? Whatever situation you are struggling with, how have you predetermined in your heart to behave?

In all things and in any situation, if you are set and rooted in God's love and know that you are a child of God, you can trust him to take care of you. You can then allow him to enable you to grow beautiful inside and out as you work on respect and submission to authority. He will help your humility of spirit (that gentle and quiet spirit we mentioned) to grow as you endeavor to have a good attitude about what's happening. In tough times, God will empower you to take a stand, not faltering and falling apart, but remaining firm. In such a way, you can flourish even as Esther did.

Chat Room

Since the lives of the girls in this book are recorded in the Bible, God's Word, and since what the Bible is really all about *is* God, I started to wonder how each of these girls viewed him. So I asked them (in my imagination, of course). The following is the resultant conversation, placed in the highly unlikely setting of a face-to-face meeting between them that transcends time lines. We'll jump right in ...

"God!" the elder of Lot's daughters exclaimed. "I'll tell you what I think about him! He's a terrible and remote God of vengeance—powerful, I grant you, but I'd just as soon cozy up to a volcano than him. I'll just stay out of his way, thank you very much! I mean, look how he absolutely wiped out my hometown, erasing the existence of thousands of innocent people. Before that, he'd had nothing to do with any of *us*, that is, until that last night when we got dragged out of town—"

"That's not precisely true, sister dearest," her younger sister interrupted. "Remember how Dad kept talking about the 'God of Abraham' and how he kept saying that our friends weren't living the way he knew God wanted them to?"

Her sister petulantly shrugged her shoulders. "Oh, that. Well, I never paid attention to Daddy-o anyway. He was always so … so undecided and ineffective about everything."

"I can't believe you called God 'remote,'" Hagar broke in. "Besides, there was nothing innocent about Sodom. I remember Master Abraham saying that God would have spared the place if even ten innocent people were to be found there (obviously there wasn't), but anyhow, what I really want to say is that I can't see how you can say that God is remote and uncaring! Look at me! I'm not even one of the tribe. Plus, I got pregnant by my master, Abraham, when we all knew (deep down) what we were doing wasn't according to God's plans. But when I ran away because things were getting pretty miserable for me, he talked to me! *Me!* Although I was sinful, a slave, an Egyptian, and a lowly girl, he actually found me, told me what to do, revealed that I was to deliver a boy, and then gave me a promise for the future! That's why I called him El Roi, You-Are-the-God-Who-Sees. This is the same

God *you're* talking about, but I'll tell you one thing: this same almighty, powerful God you're denigrating took time to deal with me personally—not like any of the Egyptian gods I grew up with."

"Well, he didn't deal with us personally," the elder sister responded defensively.

"Actually, come to think of it," the younger sibling amended after a short pause, "when the angels of God came to town to rescue us, well, that was pretty personal …"

"Yeah, well, I wasn't on talking terms with him, like Hagar here."

"Excuse me for interrupting," the soft voice of Jephthah's daughter broke in, "but did you ever, uh, try to get to know him or even think of him occasionally?"

"Not likely," the elder sister replied aggressively. "Did you?"

"Not really, especially during those early years when Dad and I were simply trying to survive. I did notice, though, that Dad and some of his compatriots were in the habit of crying out to him when stuck in tight spots. I guess that in reality I knew *of* him and realized that he was our own God, the one to turn to when in trouble, but he really wasn't in my daily thoughts. Until Dad made that horrible promise to him—then I cried and agonized and wept to him practically nonstop for two months."

"Do you think it made any difference?" Dinah, a newcomer to the conversation, interjected. "I mean, you must've been absolutely devastated when you learned that your dear dad was going to kill you, and then, even after you prayed, it still happened."

"Yeah, it still happened," the daughter of Jephthah replied thoughtfully, "but I think that change was more inside of me. I was able to go back and allow it to happen. You see," she continued earnestly, "it's one thing to be killed in a hopeless frenzy for uncaring gods in the hope that they can and will listen. I knew God had listened to us, that is, my dad in particular, so I knew he was able to listen to me too."

"How could you submit yourself to such a thing?" Lot's younger daughter questioned.

"You don't understand," she replied. "Our tribe had been so tormented by the Ammonites—oops! Aren't they your descendants? No offense intended—that we were willing to do anything to throw off their oppression. What was my one life if it bought my countrymen's freedom?"

"I still don't get how …" Dinah trailed off pensively.

Up to this point Tamar had simply been following the conversation, but Dinah's palpable pain struck a similar chord in her. "Yeah, I don't see how you can *not* be angry at God for allowing that to happen. Like Dinah, I got hurt too, and it wasn't because I did anything wrong either. I still hurt, even though I know God used what I went through to help forge a stronger identity within our own tribe."

"But isn't it awesome how God can take seemingly random events and use them for his own glory and to fulfill his plans?" Rebekah's enthusiasm washed over them like an icy ocean wave, almost leaving them gasping. She continued. "Yes, on the one hand, he allows us to make decisions that may or may not be pleasing to him, but somehow he still works through it all, not wasting anything we've gone through, even if we don't see it at the time or maybe never will, since his timing is not our timing."

"You can talk," a bitter Dinah responded. "You didn't get raped or sacrificed like we did!"

"Wait a minute! Sure, I didn't suffer to that extent, but you better believe that leaving my family, friends, lifestyle, and just about everything I was familiar with really hurt, even though I was doing what I knew God wanted me to do."

Hoping to diffuse the conversation before it got too heated, Abishag hastily asked, "Did *you*, Rebekah, have a personal relationship with God?"

"When I first met Uncle Abraham's servant, I really didn't know much about him except that he had apparently told Uncle Abraham to move away. But when he, that is, the servant, shared how exactly God had answered his prayer, down to the smallest detail, I was simply blown away by how personal God is and how he oversees and orchestrates the lives of mere individuals —you know, us small peoples! I didn't know him then, but I sure was anxious to get to know him."

"I didn't know him, really," Tamar said flatly.

Abishag was shocked. "How could this be? You … you were King David's daughter! You grew up in his home and heard the songs he wrote. You saw how amazingly God worked in his life, or at least you must've heard about it firsthand. I mean, didn't the fact that your father, the king, loved God so much and was loved by him so obviously mean anything to you?"

Tamar shrugged her shoulders. "Maybe there was too much chaos and jealousy swirling around me—what with all of my brothers vying to be the next on the throne. At the time, he didn't seem to fit into my life, nor did the heartache I and other members of my family went through do anything to endear him to me."

"Me either," Dinah chimed in. "Sure, God seemed to give Dad guidance, but in our daily lives, there was too much bickering and bitterness to allow room for a personal relationship with him."

While she was speaking, Leah and Rachel, silent to this point, looked at each other, and then Leah spoke up. "That was our fault, I'm sorry to say, daughter. We—that is, I—were so wrapped up in jockeying for your father's love and attention that we kind of forgot what was important."

"Maybe we never really tried to get to know him," Rachel softly added. "I know that before Jacob broke into our horizon, we had never given God a thought other than remembering occasionally that Aunt Rebekah had left because of him. I was wrapped up in the joy of life and the freedom of the outdoors—"

"While I was busy learning to be a good wife and how to take care of everyone's daily needs," Leah interjected.

"We were both so totally involved in our own little worlds that we really didn't give him much thought. And then, after Jacob rescued me at the well, I was so in love …"

"And I was jealous, so jealous," Leah added.

" … and that's all I ever thought about. Sure, Jacob spoke about him all the time and shared how God had promised to care for him. Plus, we could see God's blessing on him in his work relations with our dad, but we—and I think I speak for the both of us …"

Leah nodded.

" … didn't take him in as a personal God to us. I even took our household gods with us when we left your grandfather's for good. At that point he was still Jacob's God, not mine."

Leah picked up the thread of the story. "Nor was he mine, that is, until I realized that it was God who saw my tears and felt my pain when it finally hit me that never would Jacob love me like he loved you, Rachel. Then I knew that he listened to me and answered my prayer when I called on him. But I guess I never really let him change me if you never saw him through me, Dinah. I'm so sorry."

"God didn't seem too close to me either." Everyone looked at the young girl who had been a Syrian captive. She continued. "I know what it's like to hurt so much that it seemed like the world went gray. When I was ripped away from my family, God seemed *really* distant that day. Of course, my family hadn't been that close to him before that. I heard that it was because we, as a nation, weren't faithfully following God that he allowed Syria to hassle Israel so much in the first place, so I guess it's not so surprising that God wasn't really part of my life. At the time of my captivity, I just *happened* to be one of the casualties." She shrugged.

"But you told your master about the prophet," the

erstwhile silent Esther prompted her. "What made you think of him when your master was so desperate?"

"After I'd been in Syria a while, I started to realize how important my heritage as God's own people was, and the more I thought about it, the more I realized that God was still active on our behalf, especially when I remembered how he was working so powerfully through the prophet Elisha. So when Master Namaan was so hopeless, I knew that his only hope was if he went to our God. So that's why I got the courage to mention the prophet."

"It's funny that you put it that way," Esther responded. "My life was that of a captive too, though I was a third-generation one. I found great stability in recognizing that we were God's chosen people. With that knowledge, I was able to trust that he was very interested in our well-being, even if our presence in Persia *was* punishment for our nation's past disobedience."

"Was God personal to you?" Abishag persisted.

Esther responded pensively, "In a way ... being thrust into the situation I was plunged into, I *had* to trust in him, or I would've gone crazy! And time after time, I could see how he cared for me. How could I *not* trust him? And then, nine years later, I had to trust him again with my life; but as a direct result, I saw up close how awesomely he had worked in my life to use me to save my—his—people. It was incredible!"

"Wow!" Abishag breathed. "I wish I could've been used by him so awesomely!"

Esther looked at her kindly. "Don't shortchange yourself, Abishag. In a way, your service to your king was just as important. I think it was awesome that you were able to care for a man who was so close to God. In essence, you were serving God himself."

Abishag nodded. "Yes, it was a privilege. Mind you, it wasn't all easy, and it took some getting used to, but I was in a position where I *saw* what it was like to know God personally. Even with only a vestige of his former majesty remaining, still I learned so much about loving and serving a personal and intimate God through him … I'd do it again," she added quietly.

With that, we shall exit the conversation and ask ourselves the same question Abishag persisted with: Do we personally know God? In fact, what do we really think about God, deep down within us? Who is he?

Because of the experiences each of these girls went through and the lifestyles that influenced their perspectives, their ideas of God and degree of relationships with him varied greatly. By and large, when they were wrapped up in an ungodly lifestyle, seeking their own selfish ends and pursuing their own goals, God seemed very distant to them, unjust, and even cruel.

Conversely, when devoted to serving and obeying his call, these girls—Abishag, Esther, and Rebekah, to name a few—learned that he was personal and loving. Hagar knew him as "You-Are-the-God-Who-Sees"; Rebekah was willing to leave everything immediately because she knew he wanted her to; Esther put her life on the line to save his people; Jephthah's daughter gave up her life.

James 4:8 says, "Draw near to God and He will draw near to you." Let the lives of these girls show you what a difference it makes when you choose to follow him wholeheartedly. Don't be a victim. Don't place yourself in awkward, vulnerable situations. Grow into beautiful women, inside and out, willing to serve. Place yourself in God's loving and wise hands, commit your ways to him, and never look back. In your own life, what are you choosing?

listen|imagine|view|experience

AUDIO BOOK DOWNLOAD INCLUDED WITH THIS BOOK!

In your hands you hold a complete digital entertainment package. Besides purchasing the paper version of this book, this book includes a free download of the audio version of this book. Simply use the code listed below when visiting our website. Once downloaded to your computer, you can listen to the book through your computer's speakers, burn it to an audio CD or save the file to your portable music device (such as Apple's popular iPod) and listen on the go!

How to get your free audio book digital download:

1. Visit www.tatepublishing.com and click on the e|LIVE logo on the home page.
2. Enter the following coupon code:
   cff7-8bdd-e0aa-2cdb-6f52-790a-b335-552c
3. Download the audio book from your e|LIVE digital locker and begin enjoying your new digital entertainment package today!